Unconventional Leadership

Today's educational leaders are working with more resources, more research, and more stakeholders – all within the same, limited time in a day as we had a decade ago. Author Jessica M. Cabeen takes readers through an intentional journey of current trends and buzzwords, helping leaders understand how social media is a tool for connection, collaboration, and learning. This exciting book explores the importance of care and collaboration with all members of the educational community – students, teachers, staff, families, and community partners. Each chapter highlights examples of leaders that have made positive change in their schools, and provides key actionable strategies that can be implemented at a pace that is sustainable and tailored to fit your needs. You will discover a deeper understanding of the critical importance of your role in:

- Elevating the student's experience
- Building a strong school culture
- Creating small ways to make big impacts with families
- Advocating a clear message with community partners and legislative leaders
- Creating time for self-care

Filled with practical examples, tools, and strategies, *Unconventional Leadership* is a resource school leaders can pick up today and implement tomorrow.

Jessica M. Cabeen is Principal of Ellis Middle School in Austin, Minnesota. Jessica is active on social media (@JessicaCabeen) and co-moderates #ECEChat.

Other Eye On Education Books Available from Routledge
(www.routledge.com/eyeoneducation)

Unconventional Leadership

Bridging the Connected World with
Meaningful Relationships

Jessica M. Cabeen

Routledge
Taylor & Francis Group

NEW YORK AND LONDON

First published 2020
by Routledge
52 Vanderbilt Avenue, New York, NY 10017

and by Routledge
2 Park Square, Milton Park, Abingdon, Oxon, OX14 4RN

Routledge is an imprint of the Taylor & Francis Group, an informa business

Library of Congress Cataloging-in-Publication Data
Names: Cabeen, Jessica, author.
Title: Unconventional leadership: bridging the connected world with meaningful
relationships / Jessica M. Cabeen.
Identifiers: LCCN 2019035255 | ISBN 9780367074463 (hardback) |
ISBN 9780367074470 (paperback) | ISBN 9780429020803 (ebook)
Subjects: LCSH: Educational leadership. | Parent-teacher relationships. |
Teacher-administrator relationships. | Community and school.
Classification: LCC LB2806 .C22 2020 | DDC 371.2–dc23
LC record available at https://lccn.loc.gov/2019035255

ISBN: 978-0-367-07446-3 (hbk)
ISBN: 978-0-367-07447-0 (pbk)
ISBN: 978-0-429-02080-3 (ebk)

Typeset in Optima
by Deanta Global Publishing Services, Chennai, India

Visit the eResources: www.routledge.com/9780367074470.

Contents

Meet the Author

Jessica is the principal of Ellis Middle School in Austin, Minnesota. Prior to that, she was the principal of the "Happiest Place in Southeastern Minnesota," the Woodson Kindergarten Center. She has been an assistant middle school principal, a special education assistant director, and special education teacher.

Jessica received her BA in Music Therapy at the University of Wisconsin-Eau Claire. She attended the University of St. Thomas for her Masters Degree in Special Education. Jessica has administrative licenses from Hamline University in both the Principalship and Director of Special Education. She continues her learning as a facilitator of the Minnesota Principal Academy and was a facilitator of the Minnesota PreK-3 Principal Academy, a partnership with the Minnesota Department of Education and the Minnesota Elementary Principal Association.

Jessica started her career as a music therapist in Illinois and Iowa. She moved into the school setting as a music therapist for the Saint Paul Public Schools in Saint Paul, Minnesota and then became an Autism teacher for the district and an administrative intern with district Special Education Administration. She moved to Austin, Minnesota as a Special Education Supervisor and then an Assistant Principal at Ellis Middle School. Learning and leading is something she is passionate about and enjoys the challenge of building relationships with all ages – but mainly kindergarten and 7th and 8th graders.

Jessica was awarded the NAESP/VINCI Digital Leader of Early Learning Award in 2016 and in 2017 was named the Minnesota National Distinguished Principal. Jessica is the author of *Hacking Early Learning* and co-authored *Balance Like A Pirate*. Mrs. Cabeen is a sought-after speaker and trainer and enjoys getting to learn and lead with other educators across the nation.

But at the end of the day, the real loves of her life are her boys. She is married to Rob and mom to Kenny and Isaiah. Oh, and mom to Rigby, the family dog.

She enjoys connecting and growing her Professional Learning Community. Please reach out to her via Twitter and Instagram @Jessica Cabeen and on her website at www.jessicacabeen.com.

Acknowledgments

The joy was in the journey for this book. Heather Jarrow, thank you so much for reaching out and seeing this in me before I saw it in myself.

This journey didn't just start with a contract to write *Unconventional Leadership*; it began as a young middle schooler myself and was guided by a few incredible women woven throughout my life.

My grandmothers: Mary Lichty and Virgina Schober. I have always and forever looked up to these women for their remarkable experiences and how they both managed to love the life they led in work and at home.

My aunt: Donna Schober. Thank you so much for pushing me to continue to follow my dreams and for your words of encouragement throughout the years. I am here because you paved the way.

My mother-in-law: Mary Cabeen. I am so grateful to be your daughter-in-law. Thank you for being my cheerleader along the way.

My dear friend and mentor: Dr. Katie Pekel. Remember that drive home from Fergus Falls, Minnesota when we debated the value of social media and the importance of connecting learning to a foundation of educational research? Without you, your ideas, and your consistent pursuit of excellence in educational practices this resource would not be in print.

To my mom: Carolyn Lichty. You were the original Unconventional Leader. Thank you for your dedication and commitment to serving students in the public schools of Ladysmith, Wisconsin. Because of your caring and unwavering passion to serve students to a high level, you taught your own children how to be servant leaders, while having the same passion with your family at home.

And to every female educator reading this book,

Dream Big: you have amazing ideas and a passion that needs to be put to pen and paper.

Live Colorfully: push yourself to share the incredible work in your classrooms and schools.

Lead Boldly: let us create a new era that mirrors the representation of women in the field and women leaders writing and sharing their work.

eResources

Additional resources for download can be found by visiting the book product page at www.routledge.com/9780367074470. Once there, click on the tab that reads "eResources" and then select the file(s) you need, which will download directly to your computer.

Introduction

The Case for Unconventional Leadership in Schools

STRONG LEADERS BEAT TO THEIR OWN DRUM

AND ARE CAUTIOUS WHEN OTHERS DEMAND WE PLAY THEIR MUSIC.

#UnConLeader

Have you heard of a Rube Golberg machine? They are described as a machine intentionally designed to perform a simple task in an indirect and overcomplicated fashion. This past year I was taking pictures for our Instagram account at a Rube Golberg competition in our Physics class when a local reporter, who was writing a story about the competition, approached me and stated: "Have you ever thought about your leadership style like a Rube Golberg machine?"

If you were to see me on a daily basis you might have to agree. My approaches are unconventional and at times seem quite illogical. Who spends the first hour of every day out at the bus stop, in the halls, and occasionally attempting to play dodgeball with middle school students? And why would any adult spend hours learning how to use Snapchat, Facebook, and Instagram to communicate with stakeholders? In meetings I tend to be the one sitting in the back and I work hard to ensure my voice is one of encouragement and questions, not directives and ultimatums.

My approaches to working through discipline with students could also be equated to making a simple task complicated. These approaches include role playing a school bus situation, having students map up the most direct route to class if they are chronically tardy, and reviewing student essays about the importance of not horseplaying in the halls and the unintended consequences of their interactions on teachers in their classrooms. I have a weird habit of remembering odd, and at times random, things about students and families I learn while spending time in their homes over the summer and at night during the school year. This catches families off guard when I call to say we have handled something here at school and just want to give them an update, or when I make the multiple good news calls every week to 7th and 8th grade students (selfies included).

On the surface it looks like I am working twice as hard to complete something that could be done in one swift action: give teachers a directive, just suspend students, make parents miss work and come into school, and use your time to answer emails and do paperwork in the office – not greeting students in the hall.

Leading in this way can be isolating at times. As Immanuel Guy thought about what I do differently as a principal at Ellis Middle School than his other principals, he created this book cover. Middle schoolers get it; the work of an unconventional school leader takes courage, determination, and at times you find yourself on a path less traveled.

Let's Find a Better Way

In a study done by the Wallace Foundation (2009), the following statement was made: "research and practice confirm that there is slim chance of creating and sustaining high-quality learning environments without a skilled and committed leader to help shape teaching and learning."

Shaping this learning has to look different than what we experienced as a student. Think about your interactions with your school leader? When did you see them (or did you see them)? And to this day – do you remember their name? While becoming a leader in this work doesn't require an official title – it does require a commitment to taking an unconventional route to the same direction: students and staff who feel safe, engaged, and successful in their work – and love doing it.

Skill and commitment don't come easy, and it takes creative ways to create that visionary leader to sustain the practices necessary for the school's success. Another characteristic of successful school leaders we don't talk as much about? Keep reading.

Katherine Schumacher had the best of both worlds when she decided to create her interpretation of an Unconventional Leader book cover. Knowing me in my former role as the principal of a Kindergarten Center and then as her principal in middle school – the one common thread she found in a school leader regardless of age group served? Caring.

unconventional

leadership

Jessica Cabeen

Leaders and Caring

How often in district meetings, principal conferences, or staff meetings is the concept of caring present in conversations? As a school leader, in the early years I quickly learned play can be the new "bad" four letter word in some educators' vocabulary – but at least with the conversation around play – we are having it. The conversation around caring for others is less likely to occur – in any setting or grade level.

When I became a middle school assistant principal, the foundation for learning how to lead in middle school classrooms came from *The Teacher as Warm Demander* (Bondy & Ross 2008). The authors described "care" as teacher stance that communicates both warmth and a nonnegotiable demand for student effort and mutual respect. *FirstSchools* identifies "A culture of caring needs to be in place before substantial learning occurs." So if we can agree it is important for our students – why can't we talk about it as the foundation for our school culture?

Care, caring, and leadership is somewhat of a sticky soft skill, and a difficult sell with some. Without a clear definition of what we are talking about, people think caring is about surface level feelings that do not translate to a deep, trusting school culture that values every stakeholder and their work towards high student achievement for all learners. "An important aspect of school leaders' work, particular principals' work, is developing and managing relationships with families and other sources of support within the community for the school and its students" (Campbell et al. 2002 in Smylie, Murphy, & Seashore Louis 2016).

Creating a caring school culture is not resident with one person but with many leaders (Seashore Louis & Wahlstrom 2011). In all my levels of school leadership, from an itinerant music therapist in the Saint Paul Public Schools to a special education classroom teacher, to a special education district leader and a school principal, I had a critical role to make or break down school culture in big and small ways.

In an article by David Brooks (2018), he states character traits successful principals embody and spread include energy, trustworthiness, honesty, optimism, and determination. Strong leaders beat to their own drum and are cautious when others demand that we play their music. Becoming a trusted leader, regardless of your title, equates to an environment where people support each other and enhances the work of the school. Anthony Muhammad (2008) stressed having colleagues who genuinely like and respect one another creates an atmosphere ripe for collaboration.

Unconventional leadership has seen its roots in the elementary schools and now is taking over the secondary schools as well. Sowell (2019) states that successful middle school principals are in the halls of their schools, connecting with students and building relationships that will influence students for years to come. Leading from our feet, not from our seat in the school office, is essential to build the deep and quality relationships that our students, especially our tweens and teens, need to firmly see to believe on a daily basis.

Have you noticed successful leaders seem to smile a lot? Shawn Achor (2010) found that the most successful people see adversity not as a stumbling block, but as a stepping-stone to greatness. Unconventional leadership means using the art and ability to reframe situations and circumstances daily to our school's advantage.

School leaders are at a crossroads; what do you value and how are you modeling that value? Is it standardized assessments? Teacher satisfaction survey? Or popularity content on social media sites or PTA coffee talk? Creating a safe and engaging space for our stakeholders outside the four walls takes an unconventional and creative approach to make these interactions meaningful and to make stakeholders want to come back to your school for more.

GOOD
INTENTIONS
ARE NOTHING
WITHOUT

STRONG
RELATIONSHIPS.

#UNConLeader

What Is Unconventional Leadership?

To me *Unconventional Leadership* is my personal mission statement, my mantra, my guiding practice. This work is grounded in a foundation of care for others. The "others" I speak of are not limited to the following people:

- The students I serve this year, the ones who are enrolled in our school district, and the future students coming to our school in the years to come.
- The teachers, paraprofessionals, administrative staff, custodial, food service, and interpreters that call this school not just their job – but their calling.
- My peers, the principals within the district, and in my PLN that listen and support me in ways I am forever grateful.
- The families who graciously trust us with their children every day in so many ways beyond academic learning.
- The community members who are the neighbors that put up with the bus traffic and foot traffic of our students, who volunteer time, donate money, and speak for our school district with pride in conversations with others.
- Our school leadership, who create the broader vision for our district.
- Other agencies that are grounded in building relationships with students in and outside of school.

What Is "Unconventional Leadership" to You?

Who do you lead? Why do you do it? How do you incorporate an unconventional community that has impacted your school and students in profound ways? Please share this with others – put yourself and your school out for others to see and learn from. We have an opportunity today to let leadership look different, not because we have to, but because we care and we know that it will make a difference for those we serve.

Once you have your why – it is time to find your how. Leading unconventionally also means that we learn a little differently today than we might have before. Throughout the book you will find connections to the work of leading differently and social media.

> *Today's leaders can't lead without learning to use social media as a tool for connection, for collaboration and for our own learning.*

Trust me, I wasn't a believer at first. I had a Twitter account for a few years before I really started using it, now I can't imagine learning and leading without it. Are you new to Instagram? Have you ever heard of Voxer? If not, don't worry – we can learn together. If you have, I hope you join in the conversation and support other leaders in learning from you and the power of connecting with others – all through Wi-Fi.

The format of the book is geared to be easily accessible, applicable, and each chapter has takeaways you could start tomorrow. The stories shared have happened and I hope they offer you a safe starting point in your journey.

What to Expect in this Book

The layout of this book is meant for the reader to take research into action. Too often changes in education are parallel to the Tortoise and the Hare fable. We see the next sparkly new thing, new practice, new research and jump into the race to implement and find out we fatigue before we finish. Each chapter highlights key actionable items that can be implemented at a pace that is sustainable, and offers different perspectives so you can take and tailor it to fit your needs.

While each chapter focuses on a different area and aspect of leading in schools, the consistent lens across the book is the fact that leaders interact with people in many different arenas. Students, families, teachers, leaders, community partners, legislators, are just a few of the key stakeholders in leading together in education. The format of the book is geared to be easily accessible, applicable, and each chapter has takeaways you could start tomorrow. Throughout the stories there will be opportunities to connect with others in this work via social media. The stories shared have happened and I hope they offer you a safe starting point in your journey. To further guide the work the following have been included to make those connections for you.

- **#UnConLeader connections**: share other people in the work and popular hashtags that connect the research to practice.
- **#UnConLeader keys**: provide takeaways for practice tomorrow.

Leaders in the Field. In each chapter we will highlight educators working to embed key unconventional strategies into their work. They will share stories connected to research-based practices and ideas for a few unconventional traits of leadership.

Takeaways for Tomorrow. I get it … I am in your shoes. Reading something is easy – applying what you read is the challenge. Each chapter will include takeaways that can be implemented tomorrow. Be ready for a little homework and if you have any questions – please reach out! I can be found hanging out on Instagram, Twitter, Facebook, Voxer (and even a little Snapchat) as JessicaCabeen.

Social Media Mantra. Throughout the book you will find quotes with #UnConLeader. Please feel free to tweet out, post, or share with others. As you become more confident in your use of social media, start to create and share out your own using the hashtag.

- Good intentions are nothing without STRONG relationships. **#UnConLeader**
- Strong leaders beat to their own drum, and are cautious when others demand we play their music. **#UnConLeader**

Create your own! Use the hashtag #UnConLeader to share your own takeaways

Challenge! At the end of each chapter there are a few reflective questions; take a look and take the challenge to post some of your own learning and your work with the larger community of educators ready to take on a new way of learning and leading that supports the students we serve today, not the ones we had yesterday.

Thank you – by getting through the introduction you are intrigued, curious, and a little eager to jump into leading in your classroom, your schools, your district, and your community a little different than you did yesterday. This risk will be worth the reward – I promise.

Dream Big, Live Colorfully, Lead Boldly and
#Elevate every single thing you do.

Jessica

A very special thank you goes to Katherine and Immanuel for their contribution of art and their interpretation of what Unconventional Leadership represents for both of them.

Thank you Mr. Lars Johnson, Ellis Middle School Art Teacher, for empowering them to

Dream Big and become published as 8th graders!

Want to Learn More?

Muhammad, A. (2018). *Transforming school culture: How to overcome staff division*. Bloomington, IN: Solution Tree Press.

Seashore Lois, K., & Wahlstrom, K. (2011). Principals as cultural leader. *Kappan, 92*(5), 52–56.

Leading with Students

Who is our why in this work? What do we focus on the most in accomplishing our goals, mission, and vision for our school? How often do we get caught up "adulting" that we forget the real reason we have been called to this work? Michelle Obama (2018) said it best: "kids will invest more when they feel like they are being invested in." With that in mind, in what ways can you make intentional, meaningful connections with students that produce results? When you find something that works, how do you share it with others? And how does breaking the conventional mold of leadership in unconventional ways play a role in this work?

This chapter will provide practical (and sometimes seemingly easy) ways to make deeper connections with students that will pay dividends in the work ahead. Relationships, caring leadership, and authentic leadership skills are woven throughout this key way to lead with the most important group of people in education: our students.

Relationships in education are more than stickers in the classroom, more than high-fives at the door, and certainly more than hoodies in the halls. Research continues to prove the importance of establishing a caring community in the development of a healthy school culture, relationships, and impact on student achievement.

The myth: soft skills are soft and not necessary to lead. If you are the leader who gets looked at weird when connecting with kids in intentional and creative ways, quit worrying about doing the right thing, you are.

Smylie, Murphy, and Seashore-Louis (2016) share one of the four reasons to care about caring in schools: there is the evidence that social and academic support impacts student success. When modeled with students, caring leadership includes having high expectations, no excuses, and intentional ways to demonstrate that care towards students in an individualized nature.

Even movies and pop culture celebrate caring leadership. Think about the teacher who takes their class on a field trip, the principal who does home visits, or the leader who stands up to a group of gang members – with no back up. While these can be portrayed as a little larger than life, the premise is spot on. Caring is tough love and high expectations.

Elizabeth Bondy and Dorene Ross (2008) discuss the role of the warm demander – a teacher that communicates both warmth and a nonnegotiable demand for student effort and mutual respect. If we are asking our best teachers to have this approach with the students, shouldn't we require the same of those adults leading the schools?

As a leader, ensuring students are engaged is more than an annual satisfaction survey, it is deeper than the daily greeting at the door, and when done well with intention it has lasting impacts on the student, teacher, and school personnel.

CHALLENGE YOURSELF TO SAY HI...

BEFORE YOU ASK THEM TO TAKE OFF THEIR HOODIE.

#UNCONLEADER

Linking the Learning

Consequences or Punishments

Rethinking Discipline and Rebuilding Relationships

In my experience as a special education supervision, assistant principal, and principal in both middle and high school settings, I can tell you that sometimes (and some days most times) disciplining a student was my least favorite part of the job. For those of you in the role, you get this. Your investment in the halls and cafeteria, the multiple check-ins, proactive conversations, and contracts can derail at the smallest thing and most random moment. I always struggled not to take a defeat as a personal failure. I also learned that with every incident someone would struggle with my decision: the student, the guardian, the teacher, or the bystanders. Honestly it was a struggle somedays to walk out the door with my head held high knowing I did my best for those I serve.

Here is the deal. Sometimes we expect more of our students than we do of ourselves. We want to order escorts or significant consequences with that student who is always late to class, while we might be scooting into the parking lot in the morning a little late hoping we aren't noticed. We ask our students to handle conflict with students more like adults, while we can each admit to interacting in conflict more like a kid. And social media/email, well let's just say we could all learn how to talk, tweet, and comment on each other's words better.

Coming back to the secondary level, with six years of kindergarten leadership, has me looking at this in a more unconventional way. Now instead of deficits I look for opportunities, and above all I do my best to care for each stakeholder I serve.

- **Customer service**. What is the experience for a student when they have a "behavior event"? They made an error – big or small – walk, run, or storm up to the office and then what? Do students know what happens next? Are the expectations clear in the office to them and everyone else working in that space? Do you offer them time to regroup, reflect, and maybe even write down their account of the event or do you just start in with a series of questions, questioning every one of their answers, and escalating the situation?

During one hallway supervision I literally watched a "push/push" in the hall. Immediately staff separated the two students and I went right to the one I had a stronger relationship with – the one who historically instigated more of these "push/pushes" last year and had made a conscious effort to change this year. I walked right up to him, gave him eye contact, and quietly said, "let's go to my office and figure this out." At that point I made the unconventional move – I stood next to him and held his arm and we walked with purpose to the office and through 400 other students passing by us. He got into the office, we both sat quiet for about five minutes. After that he shared his side, and we found that due to some misinformation from a relative, the situation escalated. Once both students got into the same space, they talked it out, apologized, and spent the rest of the day calming down and catching up on work, which allowed the middle school drama about the huge fight to blow over before it could blow up.

The next day I followed up with that student. I had time to explain why I immediately went to him, why I got in the middle of him and any of his buddies who could have escalated the situation before I could help him solve it. And at that point I asked him this: "what could I have done differently to help you?" Completely caught off guard, he replied – you listened, you got me out of something I wasn't going to be able to, so I think you handled it okay.

A bystander to this interaction was a family member who also has a history of more behavioral events the year previous than he is proud of and continues to work on redefining who he is in the school. During this event as his cousin and I were walking to the office, he saw a lady grabbing his cousin's arm and directly telling him, "let me solve this for you today, please." A week after the event I found him and talked to him about how the experience of watching the event was for him.

Ma'am, initially I was pissed, I don't want anyone touching my cousin or any family member, but he said you have been good to him and you have always listened to me so I thought I better just walk away like you asked.

He and I proceeded to have a long conversation about how I would best keep him safe in a similar situation, just in case. Since that time neither boy have had incidences of physical altercations. Now, we still have a "behavior event" such as refusal to work, horseplay in the cafeteria, and an occasional word or comment that can be defined as disrespectful, but the incidents of physical harm are not happening and I continue to see their faces more often in the halls than the principal's office.

- **Consistency and continuity.** As a seasoned leader in a new school, by mid-year people assumed I had been there for years and forgot it was my first time experiencing events that most staff have been doing for years. Because of this perspective I have a lot of empathy for our incoming 7th graders. Three hundred and fifty 6th graders transitioned over the summer into 7th graders and entered a new building without explicit teaching of the differences in systems between the elementary campus they were at last year and the secondary setting they walked into. Our incredible PBIS leadership team created lessons for teachers to run through and we even practiced bathroom skills knowing that they left a school with automatic flushing toilets to an older building without them. These kids knew the differences of the structural aspects of our school – but not the social-emotional ones. For examples, students experienced a TAB (take a break) experience in 6th grade, a quiet space in the classroom, a walk to the academic recovery room, or even the nurse's office for a snack. Now in this new setting they pass between seven classes, new teachers, new content, and not in a clump like elementary school. When kids asked (appropriately or not) for a TAB in 7th grade we all were confused. Enter in our incredible grade level counselor. Because of the system in place where they talk 6th–7th grade she was able to swoop in, explain TAB, and offer an altered experience at our school – that still met their needs.

  Leading unconventional also means working hard not to reinvent the wheel and to ensure students don't have to navigate hidden expectations.

- **Communication.** So very early on into my return to middle school, my first expulsion hearing happened. For me, expulsions and retention conversations in kindergarten are the two most difficult conversations

I have as a school leader. Knowing I tend to wear my heart on my sleeve (and my voice wavers and I tend to run my mouth when I am nervous in these situations) I called on my mentor – Mrs. Malo. Mrs. Malo is the high school principal, the leader of the school all my students feed into, and someone I learn from daily. She immediately emailed me her detailed checklist, she talked me through the process, and ultimately sat next to the parent to explain – from a neutral perspective – what the consequences would look like if the student had a similar behavior event as a student at the high school compared to the middle school. After the meeting she had specific points of how I could have communicated more clearly (or really when I needed to just be quiet and let them process the decisions). Because I asked for help, I received advice that I use almost daily, and I learned what could happen for our students in the high school if violations of our district school rules occurred.

On a regular basis I ask the leaders in the grades above and below how to handle situations. I call upon the 5th/6th grade building and the 9th–12th grade building on everything from social media violations, behavior contracts, and re-entry meetings. Next steps in this work are creating a clearing house of processes, contracts, and checklists each building uses so I can navigate similarities, differences, and find ways to help these transitions during the challenging middle years without requiring extensive new learning curves every 2–3 years.

Leading unconventional with students requires us to be willing to ask, learn, and lead with new knowledge and perspectives so our decisions encompass previous experiences while lining up straight to the target of where they are going. And don't be afraid to ask for feedback from the stakeholders. That family that I talked a lot with during the meeting with Mrs. Malo – I called them two weeks later to check in and continue to see what I can do to help. They are always our kids, no matter how old, how young, and we have an opportunity to learn with them, and become better leaders because of them.

People to Follow:

Matt Bush @mbush36

https://mrbushlearningandgrowing.wordpress.com/

Todd Nesloney @TechNinjaTodd

Todd's YouTube Channel:

www.youtube.com/user/toddnesloney

Hamish Brewer @BrewerHM

Website: https://hamishbrewer.com/

Dave Burgess @burgessdave

Website: https://daveburgess.com/

#UnConLeader Keys

Can you hear me now?

Reflect on your own feedback loop with building relationships and rethinking consequences: How do you know your message has been clearly received?

Do you know what the experience is for a student who needs a break or a consequence in your receiving school?

Don't reinvent the wheel – learn from other leaders.

Do you know what the experience is for a student who needs a break or a consequence in the school they are coming to you from?

Have you asked for a copy of their processes?

Or better yet sat into their Tier Two meetings to see the problem-solving ideas that they generate?

Find your PLN on social media and in your own district.

Who are the five people you go to on social media?

Who are the five people you go to in your own district?

Hashtags to Watch:

#PBISchat

#BeTheOne

#TLAP

#WeAreEllis

#PrincipalsinAction

#LeadUpChat

#HackLearning

SOMETIMES THE THINGS WE HAVE DONE FOR YEARS

NEED TO BE REVIEWED, REVISED,

OR JUST DONE.

#UnConLeader

Change the Game, Not Just the Rules

I had literally just started leading at the middle school, and during a 7th grade orientation the Student Council leadership team asked me a question: "Why can't we have water bottles at Ellis?" At that moment I was so caught up in making sure all the students were in the right place while preparing for the Open House to kick off the year later that day I didn't fully hear the question.

Not unlike a middle schooler – these students returned with the question a week later. This time I was ready for them. These students walked in with great perspective, ideas, and wanted an opportunity to have someone to listen to them. They left feeling empowered, encouraged, and with much more ownership of their school.

- **Listen to our school leaders**. While in my office we sat down and I took notes, how did they know they couldn't? Was it in the handbook? Did our feeder schools have the same rules? What about the high school that they would be going to next year? In a few short minutes this group of students and I found out – we were the only school who didn't allow water bottles in the entire district. We crafted a series of questions and pushed out a survey for students and staff to answer about their thoughts on having water bottles and what challenges they could see and how we could solve them.

- **Use their words**. In the meantime, the word was out quicker than a snap in Snapchat disappears. Later that week a student I had been working with stopped me in the hall and asked, "are you really trying to get water bottles back at Ellis?" In our conversation he asked if he and another student could work on the data in their Social Skills class with the help of their teacher. Three weeks later he and another 8th grader presented clear data to the Superintendent, and a week later they went to their first school board meeting and received unanimous approval to bring water bottles back, and also took the school boards first ever selfie (that made it onto Snapchat minutes later).

Well, the story didn't end there. Later that week the two students who reviewed over 500 student responses and created a PowerPoint in their Social Skills class went on the radio, were interviewed by the local paper, and then had a TV interview.

During the TV interview the reporter asked why they wanted to help. Their response, which didn't make the interview, was heartbreaking.

"We wanted to help and was surprised she let us as we aren't one of the 'good kids'."

- **Be ready to reach out to all our student leaders**. Our student leaders need to look like the population of students we are serving ... all of them. If your leadership groups only look like one or two of the subgroups of your school – what message is that saying to the rest?

Shortly after that interview those students became the founding members of the Principal Leadership team. We meet monthly over lunch (my treat) to discuss upcoming events, building concerns, and questions that the student body might have.

Do you want to know how much power and influence they have had on the school? Shortly after the school board approved the request to allow water bottles, the inaugural "Selfie with the School Board" picture was taken and put on their Snapchat account. By the time I arrived home from that meeting, my son informed me that the water bottle policy had been changed – when I asked how he knew – he responded, in pure middle school form: "Mom, it is on Snapchat."

Since that initial question it isn't uncommon for students to hold meetings with me to bring forward ideas and action plans that are entirely student driven. Handing over the reins more often gives our future leaders more opportunities to create their voice and share their message – most times more effective than mine.

And while we can't act on all of them, you can always listen.

#UnConLeader Twitter Connections

People to Follow:

Curtis Slater @Slater_Curtis_

Laura Fleming @LFlemingEDU

Website: www.worldsofmaking.com/

Beth Houf @BethHouf

Adam Welcome @MrAdamWelcome

Website: https://mradamwelcome.com/

Tara Martin @TaraMartinEDU

Website: www.tarammartin.com/twitter-101-with-tmm/

Weston Kieschnick @Wes_Kieschnick

Website: www.coachweston.com/

Marlena Gross-Taylor @mgrosstaylor

Website: www.marlenataylor.com/

Hashtags to Watch:

#KidsDeservelt

#edugladiators

#Booksnaps

#BoldSchool

#UnConLeader Keys

How are you listening, really listening, and acting on things that students ask about?

For more information: check out Search Institute Developmental Relationships: www.search-institute.org/developmental-relationships/developmental-relationships-framework/

Morning Routines – When Vision and Visibility Intersect

*So how does greeting every student in the morning really connect to engage-
ment and learning?*

Baruti Kafele (2015) stresses the importance of leaders being where the
learners are; this includes greeting at the front door of the school. Leading
at the front door of the school with teenagers, toddlers, and everything
in between offers opportunities for independence, choice, and control
over their surroundings. Leading from the front door of the school or classroom does have lasting effects in the classroom and in positive school
relationships. Have you seen the videos of teachers greeting students with
fun handshakes as they walk into the classroom? Did you know there is
research to suggest that this interaction provides lasting positive connections for our kids? In a 2018 study the researchers suggest that teachers
who spend time on the front end to implement strategies such as a positive
greeting at the door will eventually save more time on the back end by
spending less time reacting to problem behavior and more time on instruction (Cook et al.).

Morning greetings and welcoming all into our school is not about the
leader in the halls or in the classroom – it is about the students, staff, and
families. Maybe it was a really rough night and someone needs an extra hug
or a look of understanding. Sometimes they are just so super excited to hit
the playground that they race past you with their friends. Adults don't take
it personal and be prepared for something new tomorrow. Just show up and
expect to be surprised at least once every day.

At the middle school I see the same things. You would be surprised at
the "type" of student who wanted individualized attention; they initially
just found ways to get it that got them out of class and into the office.
Once we worked together we found ways to get what they needed (a
debrief from the drama last night, a look at the pictures they drew yesterday, a conversation about when we could eat lunch and talk further),
they stayed in class and I kept tabs on them via grades and discipline
referrals.

People to Follow:
Mark French @PrincipalFrench
Salome Thomas-EL @Principal_EL
www.principalel.com/
Darren Ellwein @dellwein
Website: www.darrenellwein.com/
Derek McCoy @mccoyderek
Webiste: https://mccoyderek.com/

Hashtags to Watch:
#GoodNewsCalloftheDay
#revoltLAP

#UnConLeader Keys
Name that student who is asking for attention, and how are you finding positive
   ways to give them the attention they are seeking?

Would I Like to Be a Student in My Own School?

While Pernille Ripp (2016) asks the question: "Would I like to be a student in my own classroom?" this can also be asked of school leaders and the climate of their schools for all stakeholders. What do the posters on the walls in the halls and the welcome signs in your office say about your school?

Moving back into the middle school, my first task was to remodel the school office.

As a parent you initially walked into a room with no signs, no chairs, and no way to know what to do next. As you opened the second set of doors the first office was the assistant principal and usually a student or two waiting outside to meet with them. As a parent entering into the school there was no place for you to sit and wait. As a student if you needed to see the school nurse you first had to walk by the liaison officer's room, again visible to all and unintentionally giving students the sense that the presence was necessary and required.

What messages did this space give to the stakeholders? The first thing parents and students saw were the spaces of the people that tended to deal with students in crisis or facing challenges … so unintentionally a school with a lot of "bad kids." Also, as a parent waiting for your child you would have to stand behind a secretary's desk, which also diminished their privacy and didn't appear to convey a welcoming place for parents either.

And where was the principal's office? The office furthest away from all three points of access into the office.

Over the summer before I started as the school leader, we had a "demo day." Desks were moved, offices were painted, and new furniture arrived for the school secretary whose current furnishings dated back to the 1980s. The empty space families walked into turned into a family room. One with chevron chairs, a TV that ran our announcements, a stack of books for all ages, and beautiful artwork created by current students. The assistant principal's office moved, and our success coach became the first face our families saw when they entered our school. This showed families that we not only embraced different languages and cultures, but they were a priority in our school. The liaison officer was able to move into that old principal's office and have a very private, very secure space to meet with students and families.

And where did I end up? The old copy room. A room that has walls filled with floor to ceiling windows that faces our common area. Our staff gained a copy room doubled in size and I am able to guarantee every student knows where my office is as they walk past it every day for breakfast, lunch, and afterschool activities.

What did our administrative leadership team try to convey with all this work? That we are a school that values our guests and families, we want to offer students a safe and private environment where they can go if they have to process with the assistant principal or law enforcement, and that they have a principal that is open and available to them whenever they need it.

#UnConLeader Twitter Connections

People to Follow:
Kayla Delzer @TopDogTeaching
Website: www.topdogteaching.com/
Jethro Jones @JethroJones
Podcast: Transformative Principal:
   www.transformativeprincipal.org/
Pernille Ripp @Pernilleripp
Website: https://pernillesripp.com/
Edutopia @Edutopia
Website: www.edutopia.org/

Hashtags to Watch:
#flexibleseating

#UnConLeader Keys
What are the spaces in your school saying to stakeholders?
In what ways can you make the spaces more inviting?

HOW MANY CHANCES DO YOU GIVE A STUDENT

TO LEARN?

#UNCONLEADER

Never, Ever Give Up on Your Students

Apologizing to your students has a multiplying effect. Not only does it build relationships within your school, it models how they can develop the skill for themselves. Owning our own mistakes and demonstrating the ability to apologize tells your students: "I am an adult, I care about you, and I make mistakes as well." Returning back to the middle school, I have learned that by going first, they are likely to follow.

Sometimes our apologies don't even have to have anything to do with what just happened. Our students' lives outside of school are complex and at times heartbreaking. Learning alongside a student who has struggles outside of school and taking the time to listen, recognize, and apologize for the circumstances that are out of their control can give them a sense that while you may not be able to fix it – you can acknowledge it.

Empathy works both ways. Borba (2016) shares that empathy can give our children a huge proven advantage for success, but it also can strengthen our bonds with our children. We all have at least one hot button student. The one that just knows how to push you right to the edge, and sometimes over it. While it is critical in all grades to establish healthy boundaries of respect and safety in your classroom and schools, it is important to remind students that no matter how many times they make a mistake you will always be there to try again.

One of the most difficult conversations I have with families and students are the ones that involve such a significant behavior that it results in an extended time out of school or a placement into a different setting. While in the moment and at the meeting the family and student may not feel like I am on their side or that I have given up, I intentionally make time afterwards to follow up and check in on the family. A practice I just started this year (so for the last ten years I have been doing it wrong, sorry) is emailing a student who is out of school to see if they need help getting their work completed, if there is anything I can do to help in their return, and to let them know I miss them.

I see it with excellent, engaged educators all the time. They have this incredible way of just knowing what kids need. I watch them interact with students in the halls, in the community, and in the classroom. Giving space to the ones that are working something out in their head, sitting next to another one that needs to vent something out, writing a note to another one who will probably save it for their whole life. Building relationships and sustaining them through the years is a process that is ever evolving, sometimes exhausting, but always worth it in the end.

#UnConLeader Twitter Connections

People to Follow: **Hashtags to Watch:**
Manuel Scott @ManuelScott   #engagechat
Todd Schmidt @tsschmidty   #PBISchat
Robyn R. Jackson @Robyn_Mindsteps

#UnConLeader Keys
Try including empathy in more interactions with your students during the day.
Flip the script: challenge yourself to respond in a different way to a student and
    watch the reaction you receive.

Walk the Talk

When you are walking in the hall and see something on the floor – do you walk by or pick it up?

Boyd and MacNeill (2018) connected the Broken Windows Theory into education (the failure to address small acts of crime results in more crime occurring) by citing the change in attitude: "Sent a clear message that someone cared and, while it took a bigger investment in time to bring about change with recidivist offenders, it stopped those students who student on the fringe from offending." If we just leave the graffiti up it will continue and might worsen. As a teacher if you continue to allow a student to enter into class late, others might start as well, or worse that one student might just start cutting the class all together.

We model what we want our students to see, even when we think they are not looking. Addressing the minor behaviors consistently and clearly supports not only the opportunity to distinguish those behaviors but the possibility of chronic, unaddressed minor behaviors turning into major ones.

Tardy to class. Some of you reading this might not think it is a big deal, but minor behaviors can quickly elevate into major ones if not addressed. In our school we started out strong, all of us were out in the halls before school, in between classes and afterwards. However, if the leader isn't leading the work it can translate to it not being a focus. Knowing that tardiness impacts not just the learning of that student, but the whole class, I continue to do my best to get up and get into the halls at each passing.

Taking this into the unconventional ranks, here are a few techniques that support creative ways to help get kids to class.

- **Dance party**. In the middle school when you stand next to a clump of students and start showing off your dance moves to your favorite song – it gets kids moving as fast and far away as possible.
- **Tier Two**. I have a handful of students that are identified as chronically late to class, I make a point to try to walk with one of them to at least one class every day. We have conversations about the weekend, about the day, and I do my best to make it a positive connection during those four minutes and thank them for getting to class on time.
- **Make a run for it**. Okay I did it. One day Jason and I were at the main office doors at 7:58 and he needed to be on the complete opposite side

of the building for gym class … at 8:00 am. When he told me there is no way we will make it, I looked at our tech integrationist, handed him my water bottle, took off my high heels, and told Jason "Ready … Set … Go" and started running. Using the "shock and awe" approach he was so startled that I was running in the halls, he just started running with me. And yes, he made it to class in 68 seconds … I made it in about 90.

- **Ask for help**. One person can't be everywhere and certainly can't get over 750 students to class on time every day. If I am going to be out of the building during the first ten days of a new escort or working with a Tier Two or Three student I will ask another teacher to make sure they get to class. I have been across the country and will get texts from the teacher showing the student sitting, smiling in class, on time. Asking others to help also shows the commitment you have to following through – even on the little things.

#UnConLeader Twitter Connections

People to Follow:
Principal Kafele @PrincipalKafele
Principal Kafele Speaks:
www.youtube.com/channel/UC2Fq6
    QMwiTioZyDraWBrjKA
Jimmy Casas @casas_jimmy
Website: www.jimmycasas.com/
Mindshift @MindshiftKQED
Podcast and Resources: www.kqed.org/
    mindshift/
Dr. Bill Ziegler @DrBillZiegler
Website: www.chaselearning.org/

Hashtags to Watch:
#schoolculture
#culturize
Other Places to Check Out:
Lead the Way Podcast:
    www.chaselearning.org/podcast
School Leadership UnEarthed Podcast:
    https://podcasts.apple.com/us/podcast/
    unearthed/id1073709918?mt=2

#UnConLeader Keys
Find a common frustration in your school and find a creative way to address it.

Show Up At My …

A few years ago, our school partnered with the Search Institute to create a video for their "150 Ways to Show Kids You Care" poster that encourages adults, in small ways, to show children daily how much they care for them. My own son was featured in the video – his statement he read (and we practiced over and over) was "Show up at my games." Throughout the school year and summer that statement runs through my head not only for my own children, but for those I serve and serve alongside. "Showing up" outside of the school walls immediately enhances a relationship.

You are investing time (and maybe a small amount of gas money) to attend an event, game, or celebration for a staff member or student. Having school-aged children means I get a 2-for-1 return on my investments. Attending swim meets on the weekends, means I get to cheer on my own children *plus* children of families that attend our school. Attending middle school concerts offers me opportunities to sit with younger siblings or nearby other staff members who have children or grandchildren at the event. Our school has a private Facebook group just for staff where we can post pictures and celebrations. Last summer I was able to attend an art opening for our school nurse. Recognizing and celebrating our stakeholders' gifts in and outside of school reaps so much more benefit than the cost.

#UnConLeader Twitter Connections

People to Follow:
Search Institute @SearchInstitute
Search Institute 150 Ways to Show Kids You Care:
   www.search-institute.org/show-kids-care/
Kids Deserve It: @KidsDeserveIt
Website: www.kidsdeserveit.com/

Hashtags to Watch:
#DevelopmentalRelationships
#KidsDeserveIt

#UnConLeader Keys
Identify two ways and one space outside of your school day you can creatively
   meet, greet, and celebrate your students.

Leaders in the Field

Beating Boredom

Martha Sevetson Rush, @MarthaSRush
   Author of *Beat Boredom: Engaging Tuned-Out Teenagers* (Stenhouse 2018)

A year ago, I decided to shake up the way I was teaching AP Macroeconomics.

I'd written a book on interactive teaching, so I *knew* the best research-based practices. I'd used strategies like discussion, problem-based learning, and authentic tasks to restructure every other class I'd taught, from U.S. Gov and journalism to regular econ, AP Micro, and AP Psych.

Over 20+ years, I'd taught hundreds of students how to challenge authority, involve themselves in political issues, conduct their own experiments, and write publishable research papers.

But AP Macro was stuck. Although I was using every simulation I could think of ("Squares and Triangles," "Econoland," "The Cocoa Market," and so on), more than 90 percent of my class was still direct instruction. Lecture.

It's easy to see why. Macro is a class with a lot of complicated content. It seems logical that if I understand the concepts, I should spend class time playing to my strength – explaining them to my students. (Judging by the AP workshops I'd attended, my peers were all doing the same.)

And honestly, the students were doing pretty well. In spring of 2017, I taught AP Macro to about 70 students, mostly freshmen, in three months – and roughly 90% of them passed the AP test. No one would criticize stats like that.

Still, I kept wondering: *What if we could do better?*

The research on teaching and learning indicated there was a better way.

One of my chief frustrations with the class was that my students didn't read the textbook (at all), and a solid one-third didn't complete homework problems. They weren't getting practice with economic models – they were just trying to absorb it all. They were utterly dependent on me.

We spent almost half of class time every day "going over" problems from the day before – i.e. doing them together – since they weren't doing them alone.

I'd learned about whiteboarding from Peter Bohacek, an amazing physics teacher at Henry Sibley High School in Minnesota (who I'd interviewed and observed for my book), so I decided to try it.

Here's how whiteboarding works: the students do some sort of brief prep activity the night before (usually watching a video, but possibly reading or doing some type of experiment), and in class, they work in collaborative groups to solve problems, writing their work on small whiteboards.

That's it. Truly not rocket science.

I decided to go all in. From day one in spring 2018, my AP Macro students were working collaboratively to graph, calculate, and manipulate the macroeconomic models in class.

Their homework was usually a 10–15 minute video, explaining something like "the investment demand curve." In class, they would draw the curve, manipulate it in response to changes – like new technology – and answer thought-provoking questions.

I grouped them with students with similar study habits – so the kids who were dedicated to reading and prepping the night before got to work together, and the ones who procrastinated got to engage in "productive struggle" together.

Instead of lecturing from the front, I spent nearly all of my class time circulating the room, answering questions, asking more questions, and helping the students who really were struggling. When most students had finished a problem, I'd ask a group to present their work, and others asked questions. Many times, I asked a group who'd made a mistake to present – to see if their classmates were tuned in enough to catch the error.

Teaching this way was a revelation. I no longer had to work to keep students on task or ask them to put away their phones. I no longer had to push them to ask questions – they were driving the entire class period with their questions.

Finally, the students were carrying the cognitive load, and they seemed to grasp immediately that their job was to learn, and my job was merely to support them. I got to know them better too, because I got to have one-on-one conversations all hour.

The results were impressive. Scores on every unit test were higher. More As and Bs, fewer Fs. I immediately started sharing my findings on my blog (MarthaRush.org) and on Twitter (@MarthaSRush), and it was fun to see the reaction.

Other AP Macro teachers who read my posts started to test the waters, and administrators from various nearby schools came to observe.

I had enlisted my colleague to teach his section of AP Macro the same way (despite his reservations), and between us we had over 100 students last year, 50% more than in 2017. Our pass rate on the AP test improved to 92%, and with it our average scores as well.

It wasn't easy to make the break with lecture – if it had been, I would have done it years before. But it was well worth taking the risk. Now, my challenge is to convince other teachers to do the same.

Want to Know More?

Who to Follow:
Twitter:
Edutopia @edutopia,
Larry Ferlazzo @Larryferlazzo
@craigpeterson16
@teacher2teacher
@AP_MikeMiller

Additional Resources:
https://martharush.org/
https://neverbore.org/
Beat Boredom: Engaging Tuned-Out
  Teenagers (Stenhouse 2018)
http://teachbetter.co/podcast/
www.coolcatteacher.com/
https://makeitstick.net/

Connecting in Unconventional Ways: Coming Full Circle

Basil Marin, school leader and speaker, @Basil_Marin, www.basil-marin.com/

As an instructional leader, I am always thinking of ways to intentionally connect with my students. The word connection is used trivially in education; however, the phenomenal educator Dr. Rita Pierson explained in her 2013 TED Talk, "Every Child Deserves a Champion," connection with an adult who will never give up on them, who understands the power of **connection** and insists they become the best they can possibly be."

As a student, I can only remember one teacher who had a genuine connection with me and wanted to see me excel in life even though I was not operating to my full potential in her class. My 9th grade English teacher, Mrs. Soenksen, was able to see past my imperfections and see my purpose and greatness that lie within me. Mrs. Soenksen was able to see past my tough facade and recognize that I was displaying behaviors as a result of my academic deficiencies and limitations. She was able to reach me when other educators had given up on me. Mrs. Soenksen showed me how to use education as a platform to elevate myself to become a better individual. The way that Mrs. Soenksen made me feel has fueled my life's purpose and I have been intentional in becoming the teacher and administrator that my underserved students need.

As an educator now I see many of my students come from broken families with single mother structures. I recognize that many of my students are not afforded the opportunity to excel in school because they are trying to battle the challenges of their home life.

Christian was a student in my 9th class at an alternative education school in rural Virginia. His clothes were rarely clean, and most of his shoes had been worn through until there were holes at the toes. Christian did not care for school as evidenced by his failing every subject and lack of participation in class. One day Christian got in a fight with another male student, and once they were separated, I asked Christian what happened. He stated, "He kept making fun of my clothes and asked me why my shoes were always talking, then he pushed me so I pushed him back." After hearing him out, I told him to let his mother know and see if maybe she could get him a pair of shoes. Tears started to trickle down his face as he said, "She doesn't have the money and she always yells at me when I ask for new clothes and this is why I hate school." In this moment, I realized that Christian's basic needs were not being met and the motivation to do well in school was tied to Christian's self-image. I remembered how Mrs. Soenksen made me feel safe and cared for me even when my external world was falling to pieces. I looked at Christian and told him that I wanted to help him but that he would need to promise me to take his education seriously moving forward and that he would not get in any more fights. Christian promised me he would and we both signed a behavioral contract. At the end of the school day, I called Christian's mother and asked her if I could take Christian and treat him to some new clothes for his upcoming birthday. She said yes, and Christian and I headed to the mall to get him some new clothes, though he had no clue what we were going to do.

As we approached the parking lot of the mall, I could see his eyes filled with excitement. I asked Christian which store he wanted to go to, and he said Foot Locker. We walked in the store and I could tell he had never been into the store before and he was taking in all of the shoe displays and the new shoe smell. We got Christian some brand-new Jordans with matching socks. We also went to some clothing stores to get Christian two new outfits. As we drove back to his mother's house, his eyes welled up and tears began to flow. I asked Christian what was wrong, and he looked at me and said, "Mr. Marin, my family has never been able to go to the mall and buy new clothes, we always get our clothes from The Salvation Army or from the church." In that moment, I knew that educating the whole child extended far beyond the classroom walls.

Now, I do not expect teachers or administrators to go out and buy their students Jordans and clothes, but it was something I wanted to do because I remember growing up poor and going through similar feelings and experiences as Christian. Christian is now in his senior year at Old Dominion University and he has overcome great obstacles to be where he is today, making great grades I might add. If you asked him how he did it and what changed for him, he will tell you the Jordans were life changing, and the fact that a teacher would make sure that he had what he needed to be successful created a life-long connection and changed the way he viewed education. I always explained to him that education is a key that could open any door he chose. Christian is the first male on both sides of his family to go to college.

> As educators, it is our responsibility to remind our students that they have greatness inside of them and to push them towards their full potential. I am able to do this for my students because it was once done for me and now the story is full circle.

Want to Know More?

Who to Follow:
Twitter:
Principal Kafele @principalKafele
Chuck Poole @cpoole27
Bethanny Hill @bethhill2829
Manny Scott @manuelscott
Danny Steele @SteeleThoughts

Additional Resources:
Leader of Learning Podcast
Eric Thomas Motivational YouTube Videos
The Better Leaders Better Schools Podcast
www.teachonomy.com/
https://educationalepiphany.com/

Small Change, Big Difference

Kyle Hamstra @KyleHamstra, ASCD Emerging Leader, Elementary STEM Specialist, Davis Drive Elementary, Cary, NC

When we hear the word *change*, it's natural to think in terms of extra work, top-down initiatives, or even the latest technologies. It sounds like a lot of ... extra.

But what if we could move mountains *without* quaking the earth? What if we could extend learning outcomes without expending our last ounces of energy and funding? While we've heard this paradox that pairs well with many an academic opportunity, we also know there's no such thing as a free lunch. But there may be free dessert – and with all the toppings.

So, what kinds of experiences *are* we creating or facilitating in our learning spaces?

How are we making learning more memorable, relevant, student-centered, and FUN, while *still* maintaining learning standards in our curriculum? I believe *that* is a true challenge in education today.

I'm taking a look at how just one small change can make a *BIG* difference!

I'm not talking about the best lesson ever. I'm not talking about adding more to our to-do list. I am talking about one small change to our existing plans that can have a deep impact on student learning.

Not too long ago, I was an elementary STEM teacher on an iPad cart. I'm recalling a very specific lesson in which kindergarteners would research habitats on their iPads and then build an animal's habitat out of materials of their choosing.

The scripted lesson went well, but I wouldn't have called it a wonderful learning experience. Although students cooperated, something still didn't feel quite right. I had to do better – for them. I wanted to make it more meaningful for my learners. As the lesson progressed and persevered through the varying kindergarten attention spans, it just seemed like they didn't really care. It's that unsavory moment when the educator doesn't need a lesson plan, a rubric, or an administrator's evaluation to know that it's not going well, and some immediate improvement was needed. It was like they were detached from the reality I had planned.

They were doing this because their teacher told them to, because they *had to* – although they didn't really *want to*. Their hearts weren't in it, as if caged in the traditional structures of doing what the system required them to do, or what I was seemingly tasked to put on them. The heartless vibe was so intense, it was palpable.

How can I make this *better*? How can I make students *care* about their learning? Is that even possible? Maybe I was just trying too hard, focusing too much on what I wanted, and not what they needed – a more personal connection.

As a STEM educator, I've collected several resources over the years. One of the things I've always purchased from craft stores – they get me every time – was animal tubes full of animal figures. By that time, I had accumulated enough for a small zoo.

Now, I begin the lesson with one small change. Rather than assigning students animals, or having them choose seemingly abstract animals online, students walked to a corner of the classroom and chose an animal figure to have and to hold – for at least 45 minutes.

Not only did they select the animal before researching its habitat, they held the animal in their hands. They named the animal. They flew their animals around the room – whether they could fly or not. Their animals had conversations with other animals. And, in those conversations, some of the students realized that their animal doesn't necessarily live in the same habitat as other animals. They didn't eat the same foods of have the same needs. For a moment, the once quiet, structured classroom now resembled living habitats – vibrant with all the movements, sounds, and interactions.

It was fascinating to watch – as I did just that.

The ultimate litmus test for an effective learning experience is when the learners forget that the educator is in the room; when they lose track of time; when they can't seem to transition smoothly to the next class because they just can't get enough.

And, because of this one, small change, kindergarteners cared *more* about their animal habitats. They added incredibly *more* detail, because they wanted to. They even want back to double-check their research to make sure they were using their materials appropriately. Their eyes were smiling. The ownership vibe was so intense, it was palpable.

It's not about having the best lesson ever.
It's not about adding a ton of extra work to your to-do list.
It is about how one small change can make a *BIG* difference.
It is about how one small change can meaningfully enhance a
    learning experience.

Want to Know More?

Who to Follow on Twitter:
I'm grateful to learn from so many educators in my professional learning network. Here are six that have really pushed my thinking:
Steven Weber @curriculumblog
Bill Ferriter @plugusin
Kerry Gallagher @KerryHawk02
Melanie Farrell @MelanieCFarrell
Phil Echols @philechols
Derek McCoy @MccoyDerek

Additional Resources:
Find out more as my learning continues at kylehamstra.com
betterleadersbetterschools.com
thecompellededucator.com
ascd.org

Takeaways for Tomorrow

Seek out an office audit. Ask parents, community members, and students to walk through the school office and tell you what it looks like, sounds like, and feels like. Try to find ways to have your office match your school vision and continue to revisit it throughout the school year.

Get to know your Tier Two and Three students. Work with your student assistant team, teachers, counselors and identify the students in your building who are not having success this year. Find out 4–5 facts about your students and then connect with them individually about these within the next week. Journal these experiences and make sure to send a note home outlining specifically what you saw and the impact those positive actions have on them and your school.

Go to their homes. Connect with a student on a deeper level. Having a hard time getting a hold of a parent? Stop by the house and say hi – no strings attached. If that goes well try again, work to have four positive interactions with the family before one piece of feedback for growth.

Be seen. Find a way to share your talents, your hobbies, or your personality with your students outside of school. Don't be afraid or ashamed – just be who you are, and they will appreciate it.

Make a call. Your students can be five, or fifteen … regardless they all appreciate a positive phone call home. At the middle school during our weekly team meetings I ask teachers to nominate students and then I make the call, take a picture, and send it home in a card. However you do it, how often you do it doesn't matter – just do it!

A Few Final Thoughts

The Investment is Worth the Effort

Throughout this chapter you learned of creative ways, big and small, to engage the key stakeholders in your school. Every little intention adds up to the big picture and you have the opportunity to decide what you want that to look like. Next, we take a look at these creative strategies not just with the young learners, but the young at heart – our educators and adults in the schools.

Social Media Mantra

- Change the game – not just the rules. **#UnConLeader**
- How many times do you give a student to learn? **#UnConLeader**
- Challenge yourself to say hi, find out their name and interests ... before you ask them to take off their hoodie. **#UnConLeader**
- All students require exceptional experiences, high bars, and zero excuses. **#UnConLeader**

Create your own! Use the hashtag #UnConLeader to share your own takeaways.

CHALLENGE

AFTER READING THIS CHAPTER I AM INTRIGUED BY THIS TOPIC:

I WILL LEARN MORE BY FOLLOWING THESE #UNCONLEADERS:

TAKE A PICTURE OF YOUR LEARNING WORK IN ACTION!
USE THE HASHTAG SO WE CAN LEAD TOGETHER!

Want to Learn More?

Bondy, E., & Ross, D. (2008). The teacher as the warm demander. *Educational Leadership, 66*(1), 54–58.

Borba, M. (2016). *UnSelfie: Why empathetic kids succeed in our all-about-me world.* New York: Touchstone.

Boyd, R., & MacNeill, N. (2018). The broken window theory and school leadership. *Education Today, 18*(2) Term 2. Retrieved from www.educationtoday.com.au/article/The-Broken-Windows-Theory-and-school-leadership-1450. Accessed on January 1, 2019.

Cook, C. et al. (2018). Positive greetings at the door: Evaluation of a low-cost, high-yield proactive classroom management strategy. *Journal of Positive Behavior Interventions, 20*(3), 149–159.

Greenleaf, R. (1991). *The servant as leader.* Westfield, IN: The Robert Greenleaf Center.

Kafele, B. (2015). *The principal 50 critical leadership for inspiring schoolwide excellence.* Alexandria, VA: ASCD.

Obama, M. (2018). *Becoming.* New York: Crown.

Ripp, P. (2016). *Passionate learners: How to engage and empower your students.* New York: Routledge.

Smylie, M., Murphy, J., & Seashore-Louis, K. (2016, November). Caring school leadership: A multi-disciplinary, cross-occupational model. *American Journal of Education, 123,* 1–35 (by the University of Chicago).

Yang, H. (2018, November 17). Ellis students challenge water bottle policy and won. *Austin Daily Herald.* Retrieved from www.austindailyherald.com/2018/11/ellis-students-challenge-policy-on-water-bottle-ban-and-won/. Accessed on January 1, 2018.

2   **Leading with Staff**

As educators, we recognize that our students are extended family. We take the time to invest in them as a whole child, learning their interests, their skills, and the needs they have in the classroom, and outside the walls of our school. We create classroom rules, classroom mantras, and sometimes even class or team t-shirts. The investment of making our classrooms a family, a team, a connection, is essential in learning. As leaders, we take those same techniques as our classroom has now become a school and our students are now the adults.

In a school setting, teachers look to their class as the people they are called to serve. In leadership, school leaders look to the teachers as one group of people they are called to serve. Just like the students in classrooms, teachers have diverse needs, learning styles, passions, and ideas that need time, trust, and relationships to cultivate.

Learning today is more complex, more innovative, more exciting, and more challenging than ever before. Educators are constantly finding new ways to entertain and engage students while keeping up with the changing face that social media and other outlets play in a child's life in and outside of school. With that in mind in what ways are you finding innovative methods to support teachers that enhance growth both in their pedagogy and the impact they have with their students?

School leaders also have a very unique opportunity to have front row seats in any class, at any time. From playing basketball in physical education to testing a hypothesis in science school, leaders have incredible opportunities to see learning in action, and to be the bridge between teachers in enhancing collaboration and their own abilities to deliver content to students in meaningful, creative ... and sometimes unconventional ways. How you share this knowledge with other teachers is as important as observing the instructional excellence in the first place.

In their book *Hacking Leadership* Joe Sanfelippo and Tony Sinanis state that "nurturing relationships will cost your organization zero dollars. The investment is time." With that lens, this chapter sets a course to find unconventional ways to cultivate quality relationships with educators in our schools.

IF IT DOESN'T CHALLENGE YOU

IT WILL NEVER PUSH YOU TO CHANGE YOUR PRACTICE.

#UNCONLEADER

Linking the Learning

Who is the Focus and How Do You Keep Them There?

Everyone who knows me knows I love my dog. My phone has an unequal number of pictures of Rigby and my boys roll their eyes when they see me holding this little dog like a baby around the house. In my office I have a picture of Rigby in a frame that states *"Me … It is All About Me."* In education we sometimes get caught up in the managerial tasks that we forget about the "me" that is staring at us in the picture frame.

When building a school culture that meets the needs of your school, can you put a picture of every staff member, student, family, and community stakeholder and think of one thing you do that meets their needs? I am still working on that journey but with that vision in mind it offers me concrete ways to find ways to build and enhance our culture – inside and out of the school walls. We have changes we need to make in education to reach our learners, from the ones who walk into school with multiple ACEs (CDC 2018), to the ones in our honor's courses, and the ones who come into school every day and fly under our radar. Dr. Dufour (2015) states this so clearly: the driving force for these changes will not be fear, but love.

Connecting with Others in Meaningful Ways

With great respect to Dr. Gary Chapman, the author of *The Five Love Languages*, when ensuring that people feel valued and that their voice is heard I make sure that our relationship building includes strategies from each of the five languages: words of affirmation, quality time, receiving gifts, acts of service, and physical touch. Creating the menu of appreciation ideas that span the love languages in which people respond to only enhances your school climate and people's enjoyment of coming into your school space every day.

- **Words of affirmation**. We spend time making positive phone calls home to our students and sending them postcards, but when was the last time we did that for a staff member? Taking a few moments to recognize the small things goes a long way in building lasting relationships with staff. At the elementary level I took time in the spring to write a note of thanks and mail it home to a significant other. Teachers, parents, spouses, and children would catch me after that experience and thank me for recognizing the great things they see in the person I call a "teacher" and they call a very important person in their life. One staff member went as far as to find my own parents' phone number and *call them!* All of a sudden, I was on the receiving end of the words of affirmation and to this day I smile when I think of this moment and how much it still means to me.

- **Quality time**. Transitioning to the middle school I have found that being present in classrooms has built relationships with staff quicker than the Friday Focus, the updates in staff meetings, or my work time in the office. During the second quarter this school year the administrative assistant has scheduled me into each teacher's class for one period. During this hour I show up with a notebook, a stack of thank-you cards, and a blank slate – no observation, no walkthrough – just time to be immersed in the teaching and learning. At first the reaction was a little surprised and unsure of my intentions, but usually five minutes in everyone forgets I am in the classroom and then I start to see the calling that the teacher has been given in action. Spending time fully focused on the gift an educator shares with their students is the purpose of leaders. When we see this in action it reminds us that the heavy lifting we do to remove barriers and put supports in place for this time to happen is worth it. Seeing a teacher that was just hired in their element makes all the preparation for interviews and references checks worth it all. Having a teacher connect with you in the hall after a visit to ask for feedback on the lesson you just observed is the icing on the cake of building a culture of trust, respect, risk-taking, and reflection.

- **Receiving gifts**. How do you know that this all works? When you receive what you are sending out. Three months into a new position, I was a little scared. I had poured out a message of transparency, trust, relationship building, and a focus on student success. But was that message being received in the intention it was sent? Did teachers feel respected, supported or did the message get lost in translation? By the end of November, I received an answer. While in the office a teacher, who I had only met in July, came into the office and offered to buy me an updated style of the planner I carried around school every day. She had seen it enough to know the size and predicted the style I might like and just wanted to confirm before she bought. When what you put out in the school boomerangs back to you is a strong indication that what you are working hard to do is making a difference for others as well.

- **Acts of service**. This language is mine. As an educator I have always felt drawn to acts of service. From tying shoes, supporting families in filling out forms, to creating community service projects in our school – I love to give back. When thinking about this as an activity to build trusting relationships with teachers I found an unexpected hook – serving in the cafeteria.

  I had recently read Danny Bauer's book *Better Leaders Better Schools* and was drawn to the suggestion of serving in the cafeteria. I had seen Joe Sanfelippo post pictures of his acts of service as the Superintendent of Fall Creek Schools and thought this is worth a try. When I approached the lunchroom and mentioned if they were short servers one day I would like to help, she immediately responded – how about right now? So, I went into the kitchen, found an apron and a hair net and went to work serving chicken fried rice and pizza.

  During the next hour my relationship with the cafeteria staff, the teachers supervising lunch, and the support staff that helped out in the lunchroom changed. Within serving 500 of the 750 students in our school, staff no longer saw me as just the principal, but a serv- ant leader – a trait I try to cultivate in my daily interactions. I learned from the cafeteria staff that even though these are 7th and 8th graders they have incredible manners when being served food. I watched how quickly this staff turned lunch shifts around and the fun they have while doing it. I also saw how personable and polite the teachers are when they come through for their own lunch and the care the lunch ladies take to making sure the staff have their favorites out when they stop by over their lunch period. Later in the day during a team meeting I shared some of the stories with a group of teachers and the look of surprise was apparent. That hour in the cafeteria has paid dividends in my work with staff, and I have the hair net in my desk for the next opportunity to support and serve.

- **Physical touch**. With this layer of relationship building I look to building deep connection while communicating. When a teacher sets a time to meet with me, am I focused on them, or the notifications from my com- puter and/or the phone ringing? Is my body positioned towards them in an open stance in the hall or am I sitting behind a desk with my arms crossed? Connecting with others has more to do about how you are positioned rather than the actual words coming out of your mouth. During team meetings I try to find a way to sit as a part of the team, rather than at the front of the room or isolated. Where I sit communicates that I am ready to do the work with you … not delegate it and walk out the door.

Family Style Leadership

Working in an early learning center in December can be described in one word: magical. Between Holiday Programs, Polar Express Days, snow, and just great spirits students and staff really radiate joy during this month. A few years ago, I started to look at a different way to thank staff mid-year for all they do. At the middle school the admin team wrote cards to each staff member, I continued that at the Kindergarten Center and then added some treats in the lounge. Two years ago, I was talking to another elementary principal who mentioned he "hosts" a holiday meal for all the staff and I was intrigued. Now on the early release day in December we bring in tables and chairs from every part of the building to make sure we have enough for every staff member to sit and have a meal after the students leave for the day. One year it was pizza, the next year it was pizza and chicken, and last year it was pulled pork. We make sure we have food for our staff who are gluten-free and dairy-free and that a variety of soda and water is available. My incredible mother-in-law spends days baking homemade Holiday Cookies and treats and even has a table for decorating sugar cookies!

It is incredible how this small gesture of appreciation is taken by staff. Paraprofessionals will comment on how nice it was to remember the food sensitivities that some of our staff have so they can enjoy the meal. Teachers rave about the cookies and are reminded of growing up and having similar holiday treats. The custodians appreciate the opportunity to sit with the staff and have conversations about how the Minnesota Vikings' and Minnesota Gophers' football seasons are going. As the leader, I serve the food, make sure beverages are refilled, and provide paper plates and bags for staff to take food home for their family. I eat last; this is my opportunity to give back in a small way to the people who go above and beyond each day for the success of our school and those we serve.

How schools celebrate learning and those who help students learn says a lot about how much the school values learning (Muhammad 2018).

Creating building-wide teams that focus on the bright spots and work to provide other ways to bring people together throughout the year is another layer to care in leading. The first Friday of the school year and the last day of the year, my family and I host a "patio pd" with snacks, beverages, and time to smile over the year. In our school lounge we host an annual border battle potluck whenever the Minnesota Vikings and Green Bay Packers play. We have brought in soup and salads, yogurt bars, and on the first nice day in the spring we bring Dairy Queen Dilly Bars out to staff after bus dismissal.

Caring for others with gifts that match their needs as well as time to connect socially goes a long way in building relationships and getting to know others ... even if Green Bay may have lost one of the rivalry games.

#UnConLeader Twitter Connections

People to Follow:
Melinda Miller @mmiller7571
Blog: http://weprincipal.blogspot.com/
Principal Staff Appreciation and
    Motivation (Facebook Group)

Hashtags to Watch:
#PrincipalPLN
#LeadLAP
#EdCamp
Other Places to Check Out:
Connected Principals:
    http://connectedprincipals.com/
Principal PLN podcast: http://principalpln.
    blogspot.com/

#UnConLeader Keys
Can You Hear Them Now?
Reflect on your own feedback loop with your staff: do you know enough about them to know how they best receive appreciation and feedback?
If not, how can you start to learn this essential information?

What is the Vision?

No book on leadership in schools can get by without addressing Vision. Buzz words such as Vision, Mission, Culture, and Climate are more prevalent, more confusing, and at times more lip-service then they are of service to our school community.

As Kotter (2012) states, whenever you cannot describe the vision driving a change initiative in five minutes or less and get a reaction that signifies both understanding and interest, you are in for trouble.

As someone who has read books and articles, attended conferences, listened to podcasts, and asks the question often in regards to these buzzwords, I realized I was making it all too difficult and wasting more time on the font of the words, than what the words themselves were saying to our school and local community.

Williams and Hierck (2015) define a school mantra in five steps: simple, memorable, positive, grounded, and uniquely yours. When vetting Kotter's approach with this process the result was clearer than any other attempt I have had in defining and leading a vision forward.

Our School Mantra Simply Became: Expect the Best

As a middle school educator, you can't be in it for long and realize tweens and teenagers make mistakes. They might "flip out" over a reasonable request from one teacher, not explaining they had been tipped over the hour before. They will ask "why" more than a toddler and refuse to buy in until you give the justification. They have a group mentality that you could shake your head at as an observer, and then 1:1 they are a completely different child. At times I watch hallway interactions thinking "would you really talk like that in front of your grandmother?" Oh and don't get me started on what is on their cell phones or why in the world they spend hours watching YouTube … it really isn't logical to this writer who learned how to type on an actual typewriter, and who is proficient at using a rotary phone without call waiting. (I tell the students to google it to see what those technological advances are.)

In the day to day operations of working with this species of "not quite kids, not quite adults", it can be exhausting and challenging not to see the silver lining, not to fully recognize our calling as educators to continue to jump back up from a setback, and most importantly to understand that even though most of them are bigger than us … they really don't have intentions to harm, hurt, or disappoint us on a regular basis.

Expect the Best came out of the belief that if our students know better they will do better, that we as the adults need to look at each misstep as an opportunity to teach, not just academic, but social content for their future success.

Expect the Best is a challenge for the leadership to look at educators, students, and families from the lens of advocating for the interest of the child and to work together moving forward.

Expect the Best is grounded in positivity and the skill of reframing … and in middle school Expect the Best is uniquely something you don't always "expect" to see in a vision statement.

Each staff member wore our new mantra on our t-shirt for the first day of school … and they continue to wear it throughout the year. All teachers have Expect the Best stickers on their computers … a prize for finding me during workshop week and reciting the new school mantra.

I see "Expect the Best" on team meeting agendas, department notes, student-led groups, and within daily conversations with staff. These three words have captured an entire staff, changed how we view our interactions and abilities, and might possibly be the best vision statement I have been a part of in my career.

#UnConLeader Twitter Connections

People to Follow:
Sanee Bell @SaneeBell
Website: https://saneebell.com/
Paul Erickson @PrincipalPaul
Website: https://visibleleadership.wordpress.com/
Ken Williams @Unfoldthesoul
Facebook Page: www.facebook.com/kenspeaks
Jethro Jones @jethrojones_
Transformative Principal @TrnFrmPrincipal
   www.transformativeprincipal.org/

Hashtags to Watch:
#HackingLeadership
#Satchat
#HackLearning

#UnConLeader Keys
What is your vision? Who knows it and how do you know others know it?

Mobile Office

Participating in the #PrincipalsinAction challenge on Twitter and Voxer once a week really helped me to put my focus on kids and become a more visible leader; however, acts of service got me out and about around the building but did not necessarily translate into more classroom observation time. While I did a morning check in the #EveryClassEveryDay challenge (Cabeen 2018) and greeted each class every day, once I returned back to the office I might not get back into a classroom until the end of the day, unless it was a formal observation. At the same time, I learned that the more I stayed in my office the more issues and problems came my way. So, I flipped my office. Grabbing my laptop bag, cell phone, and notebook I sit in class-rooms and work alongside students. This at first was met by a little surprise by students and teachers but quickly became a regular routine.

Some of the mobile office duties I completed included:

- Reviewing Minnesota State Standards while watching students identify #'s 6–10 during independent work.
- Reading an article on development play skills while enjoying a music lesson in our PreK classroom.
- Writing up a coding class proposal while learning about new apps on the iPad from a friend in the Blue Otter classroom.
- Checking and responding to email while supporting a few students in finishing up color matching activities.
- Helping students get organized for independent writing.

What I have learned so far:

- Students now know that even adults have work to do.
- I am borrowing a lot of ideas for proactive behavior strategies that I can use.
- I am not overwhelmed when I come back into the office in answering emails, etc. as I can keep tabs on them while in classrooms.
- Teachers like having an extra hand on deck to help support students who might need a little extra help.
- I can get many more tweets out sharing our school day when immersed in the classrooms.

Moving this into the middle school has had an added benefit: the students are now my teacher. They introduce me to how to locate learning work on Schoology and Microsoft OneNote. I have learned, learned again, and maybe one more time how to sync my computer to screen beam. Our Instagram feed has built because of this frequent visit and the pile of papers I used to take home every night has diminished.

You can't spend day after day sitting in someone else's classroom, home, or life to fully understand the trials, the celebrations, and the past experiences they bring into the classroom. However, finding ways to understand and empathize with these experiences opens a door to deeper conversations and creative ways to not only enhance student instruction, but possibly the quality of life and joy of teaching as well.

Leading unconventionally means you have to find creative ways to learn how teachers teach effectively while taking research and content knowledge into the classroom with developmentally appropriate ways from PreK to 12th grade.

ARE WE A SCHOOL OF GOTCHA! IF YOU FAIL?

OR I'VE GOT YOU IF YOU FALL?

#UNCONLEADER

#UnConLeader Twitter Connections

People to Follow:
Ross Cooper @RossCoops31
Website: http://rosscoops31.com/
Amy Heavin @AmyHeavin
Website: http://amyheavin.blogspot.com/
Katy Phinney @katyphinney_
Colleen Schmit: @fourmonkeypress_

Hashtags to Watch:
#HackingPBL
#ECEChat
#PIAChat
#LeadershipMinute
#InnovatorsMindset

#UnConLeader Keys
Write down one way and two spaces you can lead, learn, and work from outside of your office?

No Limit Learning for Students ... And Staff

If we give unlimited chances for students to learn ... why not our staff?

I reflect on this question often when speaking with educators, working within our school teams, and at district leadership meetings. Are you creating conditions that support teachers in trying new strategies to support students and create safety nets for success in both remediation and extension of content? DuFour (2015) stresses this mindset by stating the major challenge to implementing common formative assessments is not structural, but cultural. He goes on to state that the process must be guided by a learning orientation rather than a blame orientation. So, who better to start that reframe than the school leader?

Ensuring you are spending time in classrooms on a regular basis conveys a message that you are invested in teachers as educators and are there to support what they do every day. Failing first has been my unfortunate go-to in all my positions. I have sent out the wrong link to an article multiple times (including this week), I have mixed up student names when in team meetings, and I have admitted that initiatives I have suggested we try have fallen flat. The staff I am serving with have heard the analogy "building the plane while flying it" more times than they can count. Why? Because as the school leader I have to model what we want to see – risk taking, learning, trying new things, and working together.

Jennifer Gonzalez speaks of authentic ways we can learn from each other with the Pineapple Chart (2015). A weekly graph of days and hours is posted in the staff lounge and teachers can sign up for an hour by writing down what they are working on with students. Staff can review the chart for the week and stop in and learn with and alongside students and staff in the class. The lesson is prepared – but the learning in live. Allowing teachers to put themselves out there on a regular basis allows natural learning to occur, mistakes and celebrations included.

People want to learn from and with others that are knowledgeable ... not all knowing.

New leaders, here is a cautionary tale. Do not let the nameplate on the door change who you are or why they hired you. You can't become an expert in all things overnight, nor does anyone believe (or sometimes even enjoy listening to) the sage on the stage leader.

During staff meetings and professional development, I make a point to speak less than the educators, not more than them. It is silly to think educators will want to listen to my understanding and practice of WICOR strategies in the social studies classes over the social studies teachers who are actually using them on a daily basis with the students everyone else sees in their classes.

#UnConLeader Twitter Connections

People to Follow:

Library Girl @jenniferlagarde

Brad Gustafson @GustafsonBrad

Brad Gustafson BradGustafson.com

Jennifer Gonzalez @cultofpedagogy

Website: Cult of Pedagogy: www.cultofpedagogy.com/

Rich Czyz @RACzyz

4 O'Clock Faculty: https://fouroclockfaculty.com/

Vicki Davis @coolcatteacher

Cool Cat Teacher: www.coolcatteacher.com/

Steven Weber @curriculumblog

Teachers on Fire @TeachersonFire

Podcast: https://teachersonfire.net/

Hashtags to Watch:

#30SecondBookTalk

#leadersarereaders

#BookCampPD

#UnConLeader Keys

How can you model, learn, and lead with a lens of providing development opportunities for staff to mirror what we want for our students?

Too Much Stuff, Not Enough Substance

Newport (2016) states that in the absence of clear indicators of what it means to be productive and valuable in their jobs, many knowledge workers turn back toward an industrial indicator of productivity: doing lots of stuff in a visible manner.

For me this year that has meant to implement a set of reasonable site and principal goals that are reviewed during monthly department meetings and reported out to staff via staff meetings, team meetings, and/or the weekly Friday Focus. We also created a saying this year *Expect the Best*; we made up computer stickers and posted the saying up on our school signage. What happened next? Staff have included this mantra on team meeting documents, utilized it in student conversations, and bring it back into conversations at the building level. Why has this stuck? Because it is simple. We aren't asking everyone to memorize a paragraph that they can't see themselves in, nor believe in. *Expect the Best* is inspiring, it is realistic, and it can be applied to all school stakeholders.

In education it is easy to get caught up or swept away with a Facebook post, a teacher pay teacher page, or a fun and engaging lesson on Twitter.

Ensuring that when you are surfing the internet you are certain about your target is essential.

The Power of a Personal Note

Mark French, a principal in Minnesota, makes the #GoodNewsCallof-TheDay. Every day he brings a student to his office and calls the family to recognize the great work their child has done at school. One day he shared this story of how he started calling home to the *staff* members at his school. That was a spark for me. Within the next 30 days of school I was on a mission to mail home a personal postcard to every staff member in our school.

Our human resource department sent over the labels for each staff member's home residence or emergency contact. At the end of each day I took two to three of these cards and wrote a note of sincere appreciation. The investment of time is minimal compared to the efforts each staff member puts forth on a daily basis for our school.

The response to this extra step was incredible. I had family members of teachers call me – in tears – because I took the time to recognize things in their son/daughter, wife/husband, mom/dad that they already knew. Spouses sent emails and texts back saying they put the postcard up on the fridge in their house. One family even wrote a card back to me, and another teacher took the time to find my dad's phone number and call him! The whole process takes a few weeks as I limit myself to writing only three to five cards at a time, but the return on this investment is worth every second.

What You Focus On Grows

By now we have all heard the benefits of formative assessments in schools. Dr. Rick DuFour, a champion for all kids over and over again has stated the importance of common formative assessments. DuFour (2015) sites the benefits of these are so "self-evident that it should be standard practice in every school." I hope that is compelling enough. The two works that get misinterpreted into practice are common and formative.

Setting the time also means supporting the intentional focus for the meetings. If we aren't intentional, we may promote confusion and burnout, instead of inspiring innovation and deep learning (Courus 2015). Working with leadership teams to identify needs, creating agendas, and note-taking forms that allow for creativity and outcome-based discussions is critical for the buy in of collaboration – outside of field trips and day to day managerial tasks. Teachers want to do well, and as a school leader providing a clear vision of what the focus is and how we can get there together outlines a picture that they can see and build upon.

As the school leader you need to support your team in really defining the work you are going to set upon and give them time to accomplish this important task. Dylan Wiliam (2016) suggests that if you allow teachers to work collaboratively once a week, then three meetings a month should be focused on instructional data, and one meeting a month should be focused on building teacher capacity. At both levels I have led we established weekly PLC and/or team meetings with focused agendas. The notes were taken electronically so off-team specialists and others could see what was discussed and reach out for questions, clarifications, or ideas to support the learning work. Leadership met once a month to review facilitation ideas, provided feedback as to what was working and what we should tackle next. This format has provided a consistent space to share ideas, build trust, and enhance programing for our students and build the capacities of our teachers together.

Creating a Culture of Coaching

How many times are you in a teacher's classroom a year? A month? A week? Marshall (2015) suggests flipping the traditional observation process by making unannounced, frequent short visits followed promptly by face to face conversations focused on one or two affirmations and a key leverage point for improvements. What could this look like? I have utilized Hall and Simeral's (2008) educational rounds approach. Similar to medical rounds, educational rounds are brief (30–45 seconds) and focused on instructional strategies, student engagement, curricular adherence, and classroom management. Two to three weeks a month I set a focus, created a spreadsheet, and had a set of post-it notes ready to go. I would walk into classrooms, observe the instruction, make general notes on the master spreadsheet, and give a specific note of praise on a post-it note and leave it on the teacher's desk. The first few times I started rounds they were a little clumsy and I was certainly a sceptic. What really could you see in under a minute in a class?

A lot.

I learned so much about differentiation by watching each teacher create learning unique to who they were teaching, even if the essential outcomes were the same from room to room, the lesson was crafted to meet the needs of the students seated in front of them. I was able to become more grounded in the building blocks of our essential learning targets and the level of difficulty it took to assess students while still managing a class of 25 five-year-olds. At the middle school I was able to pop in and peek over the 1:1 screens of students to see what they were working on and if it was aligned to the instruction learning targets that the teacher had identified on the board. An unexpected outcome of this process is that I am now seen as part of the school, not just a principal that sits in the office.

It Isn't Just About What You Say, it Is How ... And When You Say It

There is a reason the first part of this chapter focused on relationships first. Educators have huge hearts and many times thin skins. They put their heart and soul into what they do and as school leaders we need to take extreme care to provide timely, specific feedback that is not subjective and doesn't leave them devastated. Neither organizational learning nor professional community can endure without trust – between teachers and administrators, among teachers, and between teachers and parents (Seashore Louis, Wahlstrom 2011). Too many times to count I have made an error in communication that has taken weeks to repair. These setbacks cause the adult learning to suffer and in turn our relationships and school culture can be impacted. Our best intentions can go bad if we are not able to clearly communicate them in a trusting and supportive manner.

When thinking about feedback, Moss and Brookhart (2015) suggest that collaborative conversations should provide teachers with the same non-judgmental, descriptive, and supportive feedback that we expect them to give their students. It could be a post-it note after an instructional round, a voice message on Voxer after a walkthrough, or a personal note that you mail home. Reframing the constructive feedback from what you did wrong, to an opportunity to try one new thing, makes a difference in how the feedback is received. Defensiveness shuts down a dialogue and will not support growth, change, or trust in the relationship. Finding time to meet and discuss more concerning behaviors when the teacher has time to hear it is critical.

If You Implement Something Well, it Should Be Sustainable When You Leave

Jim Collins (2001) references a quote by Harry Truman that resonates for leaders and educational teams: "You can accomplish anything in life, provided that you do not mind who gets the credit." Setting up systems, supports, and practices that hold students to high expectations while honoring and enhancing educators' expertise is a gift that shouldn't require a leader's trademark stamp on it – but should be an ongoing, evolving part of the schools culture, regardless of who is in the driver's seat on the bus.

Great educational leaders are not necessarily the best at putting things into written practice. Admittedly most of my decisions are made quickly, swiftly, and with data but not necessarily a written protocol behind it. Recently this hit me square in the face. We were utilizing a grading system that hadn't been reviewed or updated in almost a decade. This has set in motion a district leadership group and building working groups to go out and see what has changed in the last decade and what needs to be updated to reflect current practices in grading and practice work. Ensuring leaders are always learning and growing means sometimes we have to stop what we are currently doing to make sure we have a plan in place for future leaders and onboarding new staff along the way.

#UnConLeader Twitter Connections

People to Follow:

Tom Murray @Thomascmurray

Website: thomascmurray.com

Pete Hall @Educationhall

Website: www.educationhall.com/

Todd Whitaker @ToddWhitaker

Website: www.toddwhitaker.com/

Bobby Dodd @Bobby_Dodd

Website: TheEducationalLeaders.com

AVID @AVID4College

Website: www.avid.org

Justin Baeder @eduleadership

Principal Center: www.principalcenter.com/

Hashtags to Watch:

#LeadUpChat

#UnConLeader

#ThisisAVID

#UnConLeader Keys

What is one thing you are doing well and two ways you have documented and shared this with stakeholders on a regular basis?

Leaders in the Field

Bringing the Mountain to your Teachers

Brandon Johnson, @Bjohnsonedu, Principal, ASCD Emerging Leader, Speaker, Leadership Facilitator

At the beginning of the year, I try to find ways to engage teachers in meaningful professional development. As always, some teachers are all about it and others want nothing more than to be in their classrooms to decorate and get their rooms ready for the upcoming school year. It is sometimes difficult for me to try to find a way to engage these teachers in professional development that will improve their practice. Part of my process for teacher engagement is to model risk-taking because I know when teachers and students feel safe to take risks in the classroom, amazing things can occur.

What if professional learning was focused around pathways designed to meet the needs of teachers and staff?

I set out to design an experience to teachers and staff would not soon forget. The experience would be like an education conference except teachers would have choices. They would be able to attend the sessions that best suited their needs.

The conference was designed using four components: keynotes, learning sessions, and business sessions, and planning sessions. The keynotes were set up to inspirational in nature. The learning sessions were designed to provide teachers with relevant takeaways that they could implement immediately. The business sessions were designed to deliver important compliance and logistical information to get everyone on the same page as we begin the school year. Lastly, the planning sessions were designed to be hands-on experiences that provided the modeling and practice of concepts.

We developed the schedule and released it prior to the conference so that teachers could determine what sessions they desired to attend. We kicked off the first keynote discussing our campus beliefs. Teachers then chose breakout sessions to attend based off of several categories ranging from:

- Coaching best practices
- Developing student growth goals
- Understanding the teacher evaluation tool
- Amplifying student voice
- The workshop model for independent reading writing and conferencing
- Facilitating PLCs
- Implementing maker space in classrooms
- Using a learning management system to deliver instruction and resources
- Using data to make decisions and instruction
- Hyper docs
- Executing effective meetings

Embedded in one of the breakout sessions was a live session that included live coaching. In these sessions, a teacher would volunteer to be coached by the lesser in front of their peers. The live coaching sessions were completely organic and unscripted. Teachers and other staff members enjoyed having an opportunity to see what our instructional coaching model would look like for the upcoming year.

Business breakouts for design around the topics of:

- Budget, school safety
- Facilities management
- Advanced placement
- School discipline
- Compliance items for Special Education

The planning sessions were divided into two areas:

- "One Thing" planning sessions for school improvement
- PLC planning sessions

In the one thing planning sessions, teachers worked in teams to determine the one lever that was most important to improve student performance for the upcoming school year. They worked through the logic model process to identify a problem of practice determining the root causes and developing an action plan to address the problem of practice. The PLC planning session sessions provided an opportunity for teacher leaders to see the tuning protocol modeled by an administrator and be the participants in the process so that they could understand how to implement the tuning protocol in their PLCs. The teacher leaders had time in their groups to meet with their PLCs and determine norms and collective commitments to build the foundation for the work that they would be tackling during the school year.

The conference theme was an unconventional way to enhance our professional growth. The theme was woven into all the breakout and planning sessions. At the end of the conference, we walked away with clarity on what we believe is a campus as well as with tools to use for own growth. The feedback was positive and we started the year off with a positive energy. Teachers said that they had never been part of an experience like the one that was provided over the 2 1/2 days in which the conference took place. So, what if we focused on providing professional learning through pathways focused on the needs of teachers? We took a chance and the results were extremely successful!

If we as educators focus on our professional growth, then our practice will improve therefore impacting students in a meaningful way. Our goal was to focus on the process of continuous improvement of ourselves so that it would benefit our students.

Want to Know More?

Who to Follow:

Twitter:

Allision Rodman @thelearningloop

Jeff Veal @heffrey

Jill Cross @JCrossedu

Neil Gupta @drneilgupta

Meghan Everette @bamameghan

Additional Resources:

Some blogs that I read are:

- Seth Godin's blog https://seths.blog/
- David Geurin www.davidgeurin.com/
- Jennifer Hogan www.thecompelled-educator.com/
- Edutopia www.edutopia.org/

Some of the podcasts that I listen to are:

- The Tim Ferris Show https://tim.blog/podcast/
- Aspire: The Leadership Development Podcast https://soundcloud.com/mr_stamps
- UnearthED www.bradgustafson.com/podcast
- Kids Deserve It www.kidsdeserveit.com/kdi-show

Would I Want to Be an Adult in Professional Development I Lead?

Jennifer Hogan, Educator, Blogger, Speaker, Mentor, Connector. 2018 Alabama Assistant Principal of the Year

Leading teachers in their own professional growth can be a daunting task for school leaders. We (school leaders) visit classrooms, study data, listen to feedback from stakeholders (staff, parents, and students), and we often "prescribe" professional learning for our staff. We see a need and try to find a solution for everyone. With our teachers already having too much on their plate, sometimes we also try to avoid their feeling like they have something extra to do, so we plan the professional learning down to the detail. We hope we are making it easier on our staff when we do this, but in fact, we may be doing the opposite. How do we create a balance where teachers lead their own learning without feeling like they have more than they can handle professionally? I recently had an experience with teachers that has helped me to understand how to empower and support teachers in their individual learning.

At the beginning of the school year, the teachers in our school are required to choose at least one of the school-wide goals for their Professional Learning Plan. The goals are written based on feedback and input from staff members, and one of our goals this year was to extend students' learning "beyond the classroom walls." We're a 1-to-1 school with each student and teacher being issued a Chromebook. After several years of being a 1-to-1 school, we were still in the Substitution and Augmentation stage of the SAMR model. We needed to move the needle in our implementation of our technology, and I was determined to create an opportunity for our teachers to do it on their terms.

The professional learning goal is written as follows: "I will explore, identify, and integrate technology-enhanced activities into my classroom that will allow me and my students to think creatively and communicate effectively while extending learning opportunities beyond the classroom." HOW each teacher was to meet the goal has been up to the individual teachers. Over the course of six "formal" meetings throughout the year, our teachers will share what they have created, implemented, and learned.

For our first meeting, I shared what the goal was NOT. It was not about checking a box or just using technology tools for the sake of using them. While the goal is about taking risks and stepping into unknown territory, the technology coach and I emphasized that we would support the teachers in any way that they needed us.

The goal is also about teachers getting outside their comfort zones and really knowing their "why" around this goal. We asked the teachers to reflect on these three questions:

- Why do I want to learn about this?
- Why choose this goal that requires risk-taking?
- Why do I want my students to have this experience?

Throughout the first semester, teachers researched, reflected, and brainstormed to decide on how they would extend their students' learning beyond the classroom walls. At each meeting, teachers shared ideas as well as feedback to their colleagues, creating a synergy and excitement about trying new experiences with their students.

One teacher decided she would have her students blog each week, and she started a blog, too, so that she could model the process. Several teachers decided to take their students on virtual field trips using VR goggles and Google Expedition. A few teachers planned Google hangouts with experts in the field, and our teachers of English Language Learners will be creating digital newsletters with their students that can be shared with all of our stakeholders.

The mindset shift that has had to happen has been that in the past, the "professional learning" of the teachers occurred while the teachers were in the room. For this goal, and to individualize professional learning plans, the professional learning happens outside the formal meetings. The meetings are where the teachers share their experiences with other teachers. By providing accountability and support, our teachers have taken risks that provide rich experiences for our students to further their learning and engagement.

While I'm a teacher at heart and enjoy breaking down concepts and providing lessons in engaging ways, I knew that I needed to model being the "guide on the side" and not the "sage on the stage" when it came to professional learning and extending learning beyond the classroom walls.

Want to Know More?

Who to Follow:
Twitter:
Inspiring me to take the leap are people like: George Couros (@gcouros)
AJ Juliani (@ajjuliani)
Rich Czyz (@RACzyz)

Additional Resources:
I also am inspired by several blogs, including The Principal of Change and Award Winning Culture, and I share my experiences and resources at my blog, The Compelled Educator.

Practices to Amplify Staff Voice in Personalized Learning

Joshua Stamper, @Joshua__Stamper. Administrator, Blogger, and Host of *Aspire: The Leadership Development Podcast*

To support teacher growth, we have to establish a culture of continuous learning and collaboration. Every person is unique and has amazing gifts and talents to share. As leaders, we need to make sure we get to know each person on our campus and discover all they have to offer. To amplify teacher voices and create opportunities for collaboration, I established several experiences that provide teachers the opportunity to share their strengths with their colleagues, gain new knowledge or practices from their peers, and add to their teacher toolbox.

The Creative Corner

Twice a month, our teachers have the opportunity to teach other teachers about technology. Each session provides instruction and practice on topics such as new devices, websites, or applications, in the computer lab or in our Maker-Space. The technology that is presented is geared towards increasing student learning, improving productivity, accommodating student needs, or amplifying communication. This experience gives our teachers an opportunity to explore, make mistakes, and ask questions about new technology in a safe space with their peers.

Relationship Action Team

I have assembled an amazing group of teachers, the Relationship Action Team, to implement and teach restorative practices and incorporate the principles of Trust-Based Relational Interventions (TBRI). As a group, we explore ways to implement social-emotional practices in classrooms to establish healthy student relationships, provide opportunities for safe communication, and teach appropriate student behavior. To assist in this goal, the Relationship Action Team meets once a month to learn, discuss, practice, and model proactive and de-escalating practices. By creating healthy relationships and positive interactions, we are able to reduce harmful behavior. This is accomplished by providing clear expectations, modeling appropriate communication, and creating safe environments. If students are in conflict, restorative practices provide a system to repair harm, restore relationships, resolve conflict, and establish responsibility and ownership. The four practices the Relationship Action Team learns and implements are relationship circles, restorative circles, relationship agreements, and reflection activities.

The Teacher Expo

Each semester, we provide an opportunity for teachers to share their strengths on a grand scale. At the teacher expo, a select group of teachers, depending on the topic and the teachers' strengths, are spread out through the gym. Each teacher has a table and presents on the chosen topic. For example, if the topic is on student engagement, each teacher shares a technique, piece of technology, activity, or classroom experience that may be helpful to other teachers. There is a designated amount of time for teachers to walk around, table to table, to gain as much knowledge as possible on the designated topic. Time is always an issue and it is hard to get teachers in their peers' classrooms. This experience gives them an opportunity to gain from other teachers' successes outside of instruction time.

The Power of Twitter

In addition to learning with campus experiences, it is imperative to share additional resources to learn from those all over the world. The amount of free educational content online is incredible, and we have so much information at our disposal.

At our new teacher training, we have a Twitter scavenger hunt to get our teachers comfortable using the application. The purpose of the activity is to show our teachers what a powerful resource Twitter can be. Education and teaching can be a lonely profession. Twitter allows teachers to connect, explore, and collaborate. It is often that my staff finds new ideas, programs, conferences, Twitter chats, blogs, and podcasts through Twitter. When my teachers begin their Twitter journey, I recommend they start their Professional Learning Network (PLN) by following these educators:

- Todd Nesloney @TechNinjaTodd
- Bethany Hill @bethhill2829

- George Couros @gcouros
- Danny Steele @SteeleThoughts
- David Geurin @DavidGeurin
- Jeff Veal @heffrey
- Eric Sheninger @E_Sheninger
- Beth Houf @BethHouf
- Evan Robb @ERobbPrincipal
- Dr. Brad Gustafson @GustafsonBrad

Want to Know More?

Not only do the educators listed share amazing insight and wisdom on Twitter, they also blog, write books, facilitate Twitter chats, or create podcasts. If you are looking for more educators to connect with on Twitter, check out my "Aspire" list @Joshua__Stamper.

Additional Resources:
The Principal of Change and Award Winning Culture, and I share my experiences and resources at my blog, The Compelled Educator.

Takeaways for Tomorrow

Create a one-pager. New lunchroom system? Updating your Tier One PBIS process? How about implementing writing strategies by departments? While it is important to have discussion and input from stakeholders – make sure to delegate a notetaker in the process. Find a centralized place to house the document and make a calendar appointment to annually review the process with the appropriate committee or school team.

What is your mantra? Why do you get up and go to school every day? And do others know it? Create a mantra and post it where you can see it every day and share it with others, better yet create a mantra with your team.

Find the time. Shelley Burgess (2018) even did the math for us: if you visited 40 classrooms per week for five minutes each … you need 200 minutes. Look ahead two weeks – block out either four days for an hour or two days for two hours and get into the rooms. First just create the routine, go in, observe, reflect, and leave. The next week go in with a learning target or focus – align with one of the major aims of your school (writing, reading strategies, technology integration, student engagement, PBIS, etc.). Have a way to report back to the staff how many rooms you are in every week and what you are seeing.

Set a schedule. Commit to instructional rounds and mobile office time on your calendar. Keep a list of who you visit and better yet, send them a note card of thanks for letting you be in their space observing them at what they do best.

Building on William (2016), how can you create a schedule of teacher learning, and teacher time to implement the learning? Work with your leadership teams to pick an instructional strategy per month, create ways to collaboratively learn and apply this strategy and then set weekly reflection time with the team to discuss how implementation is going and review data as evidence of the work.

Document your learning. Use a hashtag and post one thing you saw, heard, and learned while in classrooms. I have used #WoodsonK and #WeAreEllis, respectively, not only to document my own learning, but to celebrate our staff's creativity and innovation and share out with our community. Our Instagram page links directly to Facebook so whatever I post for students, parents are able to see as well. If you utilized an hour a day to go into ten classrooms, think about what you could share with others about what goes on in your school?

Sit in the front row. Too often school leaders sit in the back of professional development afraid of showing their own faults or feeling less than the educators that the learning is geared towards. Showing your support to new initiatives and practices by sitting in the front row, joining the small groups, and thanking those who have put the learning together is a great way to show your support and commitment to the work as well as your own vulnerability to the learning.

Learn from unconventional leaders. Too often educators only read books ... by other educators. Step out of the genre and into books by leaders in other fields. By learning what leading looks like in our fields you can expand your range of skills and learn new ideas that you can take back into your schools and classrooms tomorrow.

A Few Final Thoughts

If you continue to think of your school as a large classroom and your staff as students building relationships, creating common visions, and leading in a way that everyone wants to follow, you will become more successful as you are ensuring your staff feel that sense of belonging and value just like your students. Leading from the halls, from the front seat of professional development, and by serving others in unconventional ways will keep the momentum, energy, and culture of your school moving forward in a positive direction. In the next chapter we focus on our student's first teachers – their families.

Social Media Mantra

- If it doesn't challenge you, it will never push you to change your practice. #UnConLeader
- Are we a school of GOTCHA if you fail? Or I've got you if you fall? #UnConLeader

Create your own! Use the hashtag #UnConLeader to share your own takeaways

CHALLENGE

AFTER READING THIS CHAPTER I AM INTRIGUED BY THIS TOPIC:

I WILL LEARN MORE BY FOLLOWING THESE #UNCONLEADERS:

TAKE A PICTURE OF YOUR LEARNING WORK IN ACTION!
USE THE HASHTAG SO WE CAN LEAD TOGETHER!

#UNCONLEADER

Want to Learn More?

Barnes, M., & Gonzalez, J. (2015). *Hacking education: 10 quick fixes for every school*. Highland Heights, OH: Times 10.

Bauer, D. (2018). *Better leaders better schools*. Better Leaders Better Schools.

Burgess, S. (2018). Blog post: *Time Well Spent*. [Blog Post] Retrieved from: https://leadlikeapirate.net/time-well-spent/. Accessed on December 2, 2018.

Cabeen, J. (2018). *Hacking early learning*. Highland Heights, OH: Times 10.

Center for Disease Control and Prevent (2018). Adverse Childhood Experiences (ACEs). Retrieved from: www.cdc.gov/violence prevention/childabuseandneglect/acestudy/index.html on July 22, 2019.

Chapman, G. (2014). *Five love languages*. Chicago, IL: Northfield Publishing.

Collins, J. (2001). *Good to great*. Quote cited by McCullough, David (1992) in *Truman*. New York: Simon and Schuster.

Couros, G. (2015). *The innovator's mindset*. San Diego, CA: Dave Burgess Consulting, Inc.

DuFour, R. (2015). *In praise of American educators: And how they can become even better*. Bloomington, IN: Solution Tree Press.

Hall, P., & Simeral, A. (2008). *Building teachers' capacity for success*. Alexandria, VA: ASCD.

Marshall, K. (2015, August). How principals can reshape the teaching bell curve. *The Professional Learning Journal, 36*(4), 34–37. Retrieved from https://learningforward.org/journal/august-2015-issue/how-principals-can-reshape-the-teaching-bell-curve/ on July 22, 2019.

Moss, C., & Brookhart, S. (2015). *Formative classroom walkthroughs: How principal and teachers collaborate to raise student achievement*. Alexandria, VA: ASCD.

Muhammad, A. (2018). *Transforming school culture: How to overcome staff division.* Bloomington, IN: Solution Tree Press.

Sanfelippo, J., & Sinanis, T. (2016). *Hacking leadership.* Highland Heights, OH: Times 10.

Seashore Lois, K., & Wahlstrom, K. (2011). Principals as cultural leaders. *Kappan, 92*(5), 52–56.

Newport, C. (2016). *Deep work: Rules for focused success in a distracted world.* New York: Grand Central Publishing.

William, D. (2016). *Leadership for teacher learning.* West Palm Beach, FL: Learning Sciences International.

Williams, K., & Hierck, T. (2015). *Starting a movement: Building culture from the inside out in professional learning communities.* Bloomington, IN: Solution Tree Press.

3

Leading with Family Members

Have you had that family? You know the one who goes right to the top with their concerns and skips all the rungs of the ladder? As a leader in the classroom and the school, working through conflict without racing up the escalation ladder is a challenge. Unconventional leadership in the classroom and the office when working with families requires rethinking "right" vs "wrong" and instead looking for middle ground, perspective taking, and true listening to make a real difference.

How are you already shining a spotlight on family members when they come into your school, drop off their children in the morning, or arrive at the end of the day for parent pickup? Your actions speak volumes and being absent when opportunities to build relationships with parents are presented impacts current and future relationships.

Parent relationships no longer come in the form of two to three times per year in a conference format. Offering more ways to engage than Dads and Donuts or the twice a year conferences means you have to look at what your school families can offer you and what you might need from them. Deep relationships can occur in homes, grocery stores, churches, or Saturday volleyball tournaments.

In this chapter we will look at the barriers to creating authentic parent relationships. What hasn't worked and what might if you tried. And unconventionally introducing the impact that a strong, positive social media presence could have on your school community.

WHAT IF WE INVESTED TIME IN OUR CHILDREN

TWO-THREE YEARS BEFORE THEY BECAME OUR STUDENTS?

#UNCONLEADER

Linking the Learning

Hold the Baby, Hug the Toddler, High Five the Tweener, Give the High Schooler a Handshake

Routines and rituals are the foundation in education. We all use them and lean on them to establish trust, build a sense of security, and support/scaffold student learning through the use of them. Routines can also set the stage for unconventional family engagement.

At the end of every school day each of our teachers walks their class of students to the bus, and then we all wait until everyone is on the right bus, or with their families before we wave goodbye to the buses. Rain, sleet, snow, or 30 degrees below – this is our routine. This is how we show families we care for their kids outside of those four walls. This is how we celebrate and send off our students every day.

During this daily routine I met a friend. She waited with her mom every day for her older brother to come out of the school. I noticed she always had the most stylish boots and her hair was always up in adorable pigtails. Every day I made a point to go over, bend down, and talk with her. Mid-year we moved up in our relationship and I would pick her up and/or have her walk with me a little bit while we waited for big brother. She had become such a part of my day that at a parent night I introduced her to my own family since we talk so much about her. Fast forward a few years, as the middle school principal on the first day of school I was out at parent drop off with a large group of teachers, and a solid sound system welcoming all the students into school for a new year. As one car pulled up, I saw a mom waving me over. I was unsure of what I was walking up to until the back window rolled down and I saw those familiar pigtails, two years later! My little friend had a big, big brother that was now in the middle school! What if we celebrated and invested that much time with students 2–3 years before they set foot into our school? How excited would elementary students be to see the middle or high school principals eat lunch with them? What about the 4th grade teachers hanging out during recess with the K/1/2 kids? Celebrity status – check.

School registration events can be a stressful process for families. Making sure you have the right forms filled out, birth certificates and vaccination records completed, setting up back to school conferences … all while hoping your child is enjoying their first school experience is nerve racking. Staff always know right where to find me during these events … holding someone's baby. Think about it – moms and dads don't have enough hands as it is. Add in trying to turn in paperwork while waiting in line with infants' and toddlers' families and it can become so nervous and stressful – the last thing we want this time to be for families.

Being patient and available is key to help provide comfort during this process, almost like a weighted blanket for families.

One time I was so caught up in playing with an infant and three-year-old, I was almost late to a teacher interview I had scheduled. But when I arrived at the office – what a tone that set.

Sorry I am running a few minutes late for your interview (while holding a two-week-old baby), would you mind waiting just about ten more minutes while this little guy's mom and I finish our paperwork for school next year?

Sharing that our school mission and passion for families is a priority in such an authentic way showed that future teacher (yup, we hired her) that we prioritize our learners in many, many different ways.

Making sure that the other kids in the family equation feel just as equally important as the student(s) in your school help to solidify a foundation of 'all students' matter, no matter how old … no matter how young.

Do you know much about fidget spinners, Snapchat, Instagram or the newest action movies? For siblings, finding a way to connect while they wait in your school helps to establish a relationship with a key stakeholder – a role model for younger students. I also look to these opportunities as ways to put my best self forward so when school gets tough kids know there is an ally on their side.

For the past ten years I have volunteered at our high school commencement ceremony. When I was working at the middle and high school, this was my "clouds are clearing" moment after the end of the year … see they do graduate and some of them remember you somewhat in a positive light! When waiting downstairs with nervous and excited seniors I have a captive audience to ask important questions. Yes, I do ask the staples: "What is next?" "What are you looking forward to in your journey?" but this is also an opportunity for me to gain feedback from previous students.

- What do you remember about your younger school years?
- What did you like about those days?
- What did you learn in kindergarten that still holds true now?

While these seniors are anxiously waiting to walk down the aisle, they are willing to open up and share their stories with me … I mean at this point what can they lose with their honesty? And I am only able to gain valuable information that can make school more enjoyable for future graduates.

Ask Them for Help

Sir Ken Robinson (2015) agrees: "If a parent or another member of the community can supplement what the school is offering, everyone wins." So instead of dismissing or diminishing what a parent is bringing to the table in a conversation think about how you can enhance and support what they say. Challenge yourself to think outside of the parent not just being a parent, but a person. What unique gifts do they have that could contribute to the school.

We have asked parents that are tech savvy to help us enhance our digital footprint and look over our website. A local chiropractor has volunteered to help students access sports physicals so they can be eligible for 7th–12th grade sports and activities. Other parents have donated or offered goods from their stores and restaurants at a significantly reduced rate, just because we asked. Another parent, and an incredible mother, has helped to redecorate and redesign our school offices to make them more welcoming and inviting.

I have asked parents to come in and speak to staff in regard to the unique role they play in our community. They might be a refugee from Sudan, or an immigrant from another country, but their expertise and experiences are better than any book, blog, or podcast I could share. Staff have always come back and been grateful for the enhancement a parent makes to our professional development and it always enhances the relationships that we have formed.

How are you celebrating the good with families?

When I was at the kindergarten center, I started writing positive notes home to every student after a classroom visit within the first month of school (Cabeen 2018). Moving into the secondary world this took on a new approach. During our weekly team meetings, the teachers identified a student who they wanted to recognize. It could be for making a significant positive change, it could have been because of an interaction, and it could be just for a student who comes to class every day doing their job. The criteria cast a wide net so all students could be caught in it during the year. The piece of this process that has been the most impactful for me is the call home to the parent. After the student comes to the office and takes the selfie, we contact a parent. Putting them on speakerphone and watching the child's reaction is priceless! We make the calls when we have an interpreter available, so language is no barrier for sharing joy. Responses from the parent have ranged from tears to shock. However, the calls that have meant the most are the ones that have identified a student who just flies under the radar. We all have them, actually they are usually about 60% of the class. These students come in everyday, on time, turn in their work, and go to the next class. When these parents are contacted surprise is the reaction. Wait, what, are they okay? We have never had a call from school before. And in the end "thank you so much for calling us – we love hearing that you see at school what we see at home."

> Parents need to know that their child will be loved and cared for at a deep level before they hear anything else you have to say. Sometimes how you say it, and how often makes more of a difference to them than anything else you do in a school year. #UnConLeader

Taking these new layers into consideration we started to ask our families, "what could we do different?" when planning events that are opportunities for us to put our best foot forward. Because of this feedback we completely overhauled our Kindergarten Registration Event. Families are sent a lot of information up front in regard to the process; this gives families time to read and review at home – not in a long line. We created a "What to Expect" video that walks families through what will happen at each table when they arrive for the event. When parents come in for the introduction, we give them handouts with all the information (before this we just expected parents to remember all the dates) that I go over during the presentation. We also shortened the presentation by half so we could spend time introducing staff and sharing our kindergarten readiness videos with families so they had a better understanding of the concepts that they could work on at home to help their child feel more confident and prepared for kindergarten in the fall.

Now when we plan events, we think through the following:

- Did I schedule these events around when families might work? (i.e. 1st shift vs 2nd or 3rd shift)
- Will this event add value to the family's school experience? Is the information we want to share best presented in person or in a different format (videos/social media/newsletters)?
- Can I capitalize on community events to get our message out? (Attend library events, preschool family nights, community celebrations)

- How can I include other family members in feeling welcome in our school? For example, during our registration events we have a sibling room for siblings to hang out in while parents are in my session and their siblings are in the kindergarten room.

SOMETIMES
HOW YOU SAY IT,
AND HOW
OFTEN

MAKES MORE OF A
DIFFERENCE TO THEM THAN
ANYTHING ELSE YOU DO
IN A SCHOOL YEAR.

#UnConLeader

#UnConLeader Twitter Connections

People to Follow:
Search Institute @SearchInstitute
Website: www.search-institute.org/
Parent Camp @ParentCamp
Website: www.parentcamp.org/

Hashtags to Watch:
#developmentalrelationships
#PTAs
#parentedcamp

#UnConLeader Keys

In what ways are you intentionally, and unconventionally, listening to your parents' voice?

How are you building and sustaining relationships with tweens, teens, and toddlers?

Band-Aids and Bruises: When the Rough Stuff Happens

In education we have the opportunity to walk alongside families and other educators in the midst of immense joy and happiness of life. And occasionally we have the opportunity to also walk alongside these same families during the darker times.

If I could define one student who really shaped who I am as a principal, teacher, and parent it would have to be Sam. He is my kindergarten to career student who at times became more like a son. And you didn't get to know Sam without meeting his guardian, Ellie. Ellie was kind of a bulldog ... she had high expectations for anyone who came in contact with her baby and had strong rationale for having her guard up. In his young life he endured more than most adults could handle, and under Ellie's care he was healing from bruises on the inside and out. During our first two years together, I learned so much about having empathy and high expectations for a child through Ellie. She expected so much from him and didn't let his history define or diminish what she knew he was capable of becoming. He became more than just a student, but part of our extended family. While on maternity leave, I would go to his house after school with our baby so he could meet and read stories to him. As my son grew up, in the summers we would have play dates in their living room with the huge tubs of Thomas the Trains swallowing them both up for hours of fun.

During Sam's 3rd–6th grade school years we experienced transitions. I moved for a new career and he switched schools and special education case managers. During this time, we kept in contact through letters and phone calls. I was no longer an educator, but an advocate for him and Ellie. Helping to find resources, seeking supports, or just listening after another bad day for him. I learned from them that teaching (and leading) doesn't end when the bell rings – or their school location changed.

The biggest transition was yet to come; I can still remember seeing Ellie's number on my cell phone and stepping out of my lunchroom duties as an assistant principal two hours away. Thinking it was an update from a recent IEP, I was not prepared for what she had to say. "Jessie – the cancer is back – I need you to come up here and tell Sam I am dying." For the next three months my immediate family in Austin, Minnesota made multiple trips back to Saint Paul to be with our "extended family." We sat with Ellie, and took Sam to the zoo. And when she passed away, I had the honor of giving a eulogy for this woman who was no longer a parent, but a friend, a mentor, and an incredible woman who I will never forget.

A few years ago, I went to Sam's high school graduation party. He and his guardian paraded me around like I was royalty. "Everyone, this is Miss Jessica, Sam's kindergarten teacher", they would say. This young man, his Ellie, and all those around him taught me about showing up for the rough stuff. And that sometimes your teacher becomes part of your family.

Getting it Right the Second Time

Leading and living in the same community provides you so many opportunities to build connections with families outside of the 8:00am–3:00pm school day. Switching leadership positions within the same district can also accomplish the same concept. In my time in the Austin Public Schools I slid backwards in the ages/grades of students I served. I started as the middle/high school special education supervisor working with students from 6th grade through to age 21. This age group had a focus on workforce readiness, supporting families through the transitions between middle/high school, and high school/post-secondary. We had to have tough meetings about discipline, graduation requirements, and guardian/conservatorship discussions for students whose abilities might make them vulnerable as adults. As a middle school assistant principal, I built on relationships with older siblings to gain trust as quickly as I could so conversations in the hallway weren't seen as "out to get you" but "want to learn more about you."

One family in particular has spanned every role I have had in the district for the past 11 years. Between the eight children in the family, at the current count I have worked with five of them closely. Between building relationships at school to help them see allies and not enemies with the adults in school to supporting the family when their stepmom arrived from Africa with their baby brother I knew more about them than most other families. I visited their home on a regular basis and did my best to help mom transition to America while dad was working for his degree.

Five years later I watched one of the boys walk across the stage at our high school and graduate and the next year that baby who I met when he arrived in America became my student at the kindergarten center. The excitement and relief that family had seeing me open the car door on the first day of parent drop off made all the efforts of pouring in completely worth the work.

In those five years, three of the boys I had worked with made choices that had them in and out of prison and juvenile detention centers. While dad continued his studies and hoped to instill the success of an American education, some of his children were turning to drugs, violence, and the other side of the American life he didn't want them to see. Having a deep relationship with this family from middle school helped me to really know the expectations they had on this young man and how important his success was to their family and the spirit of the dream they had for their life in America. Two years later I read in the paper one of the boys from the middle school had been arrested for armed robbery and assault; two days later his dad passed away. Going to a funeral for a family in the midst of such loss and sadness is a memory I will not forget. Having the opportunity to continue to pour into the boys in the schools I serve is a blessing I do not take for granted. Six months after the funeral the next child in the family became a kindergarten student in our school. With his new life circumstances, I took extra care for this young man. We met as a team in May with his preschool teachers to ensure we placed him with the right supports in place, I visited with mom and the church members who were supporting her during this time of loss to ensure she had what she needed for all the kids to start school. We worked with the school district to update emergency contacts and found ways to help get information home in her home language and within ways that she was able to understand.

Shortly into the school year the trauma and loss caught up to the student, aggressive behaviors started to pop up, and phone calls were more frequently made; that is when we tried a little unconventional family approach to supporting him. With the loss of his dad, and his other brothers being arrested (two more within this window of time), we decided to give him a chance to connect with a few positive male role models. One of the community elders in the Sudanese community started to come in and met with the student, and then I pulled in the big guy – my husband. Rob works as a welder for a utility company, he had met the older boys when I worked in the middle school and he had met dad on multiple occasions in the community. As a team we set a goal and then put in place regular lunch visits between Rob and the student. In between chicken sandwiches and French fries they played games, read books, and built a relationship in which the student could see that even though his dad was gone, there were other men in the community that wanted to carry on his dad's vision for his success.

Now this student is in first grade and I get regular updates from his 8th grade cousin on his success, and sometimes that cousin brings the kids to events so I can see them and give them big hugs until the smile I saw in kindergarten pops back up. This past week both boys had a holiday concert that we hosted in our middle school and guess who ran right up to both of them and gave them hugs?

While I can't go back in time and pour into the older siblings and work harder to prevent the hardships they are going through, I will be relentless in ensuring their younger siblings know that the school is a safe place that houses many caring adults for them to lean on.

Have You Achieved Celebrity Status?

I lead where I live and love every single moment of it. Living in a community of about 24,000 people offers you a type of celebrity status I would have never seen in the bigger cities I taught in prior to moving down to Southeastern Minnesota. You can never really go anywhere without knowing someone – so be prepared and be "on" for the kids and parents you serve.

Here are a few examples of what I see on a regular basis:

- On my Saturday morning long runs I will get cheers and waves in the native languages of the families and students I serve when running downtown.
- Sunday mornings at church I have my own section of groupies when I come off the stage from playing drums who are waving, smiling, and nudging their parents (hey, that is MY principal!).
- Going to the grocery store is an added celebrity status (and 45 minutes to our trip – sorry, honey) as kids will run up and hug, parents will stop

to say hi and former students love to tell me how things are going for them now.

- Actually, shopping anywhere. A lot of my former students work in town so I can connect with them and we talk "the old days." Once a former student retold a time of how I suspended him to my husband; in his words "but besides that one time she really wasn't a bad assistant principal."

- You can become a GrandPrincipal or GrandTeacher. This past year I was invited over to meet two of my former students' newborn baby. I love watching the young man I knew so well in middle school grow into such a kind, caring, and responsible adult and can't wait till my little GrandPrincipal baby comes to my school in a few years.

- Okay – truth be told – I have generations of students already. It is incredible to watch a first-generation relationship deepen when they bring their children to your school. It also gives me time to reconnect and find out how the parents are, what they are doing, and to make sure I tell them how proud I am of them and how grateful I am for them letting me have their children in our school.

Even if you live a few miles away, or your school district and city is so big, these examples wouldn't be possible without finding space outside of your school and school day to attempt to connect in some small way with one family and watch that experience pay dividends in both sides of the relationship.

The moment you tell me that you know my child is the moment I know you don't.

Please be cautious about the tone and information you share with parents. At times educators can accidently come off as the "expert" of parents' children. It is important to ensure communication is layered with "we" statements, not "me" statements. If a parent states something, the first words out of your mouth to respond shouldn't be to criticize or show your own expertise, they should be to acknowledge and build upon the statement.

IF I AM
AFRAID TO GO
INTO THEIR
HOMES

HOW CAN I BE A FEARLESS LEADER AND ADVOCATE FOR THEIR SUCCESS.

#UnConLeader

#UnConLeader Twitter Connections

People to Follow: **Hashtags to Watch:**
Joe Mazza @Joe_Mazza   #screenagers
Dr. Michele Borba @Micheleborba
Website: http://micheleborba.com/
Dr. Terrie Rose: www.drterrierose.com/
Screenagers Movie @ScreenagerMovie
Website: www.screenagersmovie.com/

#UnConLeader Keys

Reflect on a time in which a parent communication and interaction could have
    gone differently? What would you do differently now, or how can you fix it?
Ask parents "what could we do differently?"
Then do that.

Where is Your Feedback Loop?

So, you did the student survey at the beginning of the year, you met with the parents, and found out their child's favorite activities. But what are you doing with this knowledge on a regular basis?

Teenagers want to be heard and acknowledged, even (or especially) the difficult ones (Rush 2018). Kids need to see intentional interactions and a deep sense of care from the teacher on a regular basis to really believe what they are seeing. That the adult cares, believes in, and works with them to achieve their hopes and dreams.

When I came back to the middle school, many people thought I was … well, crazy. Besides switching age levels there was some push back on what I did in the early grades and how that would translate to the upper grades. Home visits was on the top of the list. In the elementary grades, and more specifically the preschool ages, home visits are a natural part of the school-home relationship. But in middle school?

During my interview for the position I shared an idea. I wanted to visit the homes of 20 students who, based upon multiple data points and feedback from staff, had a negative school experience. So, starting in August I went out and knocked on doors with my business card in hand. Each visit was met with a wall from the parent and a face of shock by the incoming 7th/8th grader. But after a few minutes of conversation and reassurance I was not at their home for anything negative, the wall came down, the door opened a little wider, and I was able to come into the house.

After those 20 home visits I sent a handwritten note and my business card again thanking them for the visit and to let me know if they needed anything before the school year started. I made a point to connect with these families again at school registration, 7th grade orientation, summer football practice, and the back to school conference. My goal – 2 positive interactions with these 20 students before the school year started. Once the year started, the final 20 came into play. With the amazing skills of the incredible administrative assistant, I was scheduled into one of each of these students' classes for 20 minutes. During this time, I just quietly snuck in, sat by them, and asked how things were going. Reflecting back on this experience I had quite the range of comments. One of my favorites was at the school registration when I ran into a student I saw at his home the week before where he looked at me and said "Whoa, you really *ARE* my new principal." Students told me they received my card and one even said they had it up in their room. Two of those students were able to get registered for Fall Sports because of the home visits, one family was able to get an IEP meeting scheduled to check on accommodations, another student was able to see that I wasn't as bad as they thought as their younger siblings ran up to me in the home and hugged me as their former kindergarten principal.

Back in the school setting, even though I was the newest person to the school, I had detailed information on students who were most likely to have the hardest time being successful during the year. I was able to share this information with the teachers – down to where the parents worked and when their shift started so teachers could connect with them in a timely manner. These identified students also made it into our team conversations during the first month of school so I could get a sense of how they were doing in class, even when I wasn't in the seat next to them.

We are now into the second semester of this school year and one of those students has had ZERO behavioral referrals! Many of the 20 students have seen positive changes in their grades, attendance, and behavior referrals. And in talking with their parents throughout the year – this year is going better for them as well than last year. Mid-year we also celebrated this update with the teachers and took time to pause and celebrate the success of these students' social-emotional growth. When I started knocking on those doors, my purpose was to be a friendly face. Looking back that first step turned into a lot more.

Have You Made a Connection Outside of the School Walls?

In my educational career I have been blessed to walk alongside a few families through tremendous suffering, pain, and loss in their life. These experiences have given me opportunities to build my understanding, perspective, and relationships with families – especially those whose cultures and life experiences are different than my own. I have been at funerals of family members in which the entire service is spoken in their native tongue. I have been fortunate to attend the Karen Martyr Day and Wrist Tying Festival in Austin, Minnesota two years in a row and meet extended family of the students I serve. During the school year the secretary makes sure I attend at least one event of all the different groups we have in our school. From basketball games, chess club, musicals, and math league – finding ways to interact with parents on their terms and within their own strengths and passions forges a deeper relationship than ever before.

#UnConLeader Twitter Connections

People to Follow:
Jay Posick @posickj
Families and Schools Together @FASTcommunity
Website: www.familiesandschools.org/our-organization/
#UnConLeader Keys
Attend an event outside your school that impacts your families. Make sure to interact with the families that you serve and connect with your students when you see them back at school the next day.

Leaders in the Field

Creating a Community Rooted in Parent Involvement

Karine Veldhoen, School Administrator, Author, Humanitarian, @Mrs_KV

Parents are the most under-leveraged resource in schools! In my experience in schools in two States and two Canadian Provinces, parents and guardians want the best for their child almost universally. As educational leaders, we have a unique opportunity to harness and leverage the potential of parents to inspire and empower personalized learning for children.

As a parent myself, I know first-hand how great the pressures of parenting, careers, home-making, and sustaining healthy family relationships are. I have three children spanning 15 years, so I will be an on-duty mom for 33 years. Being a mom calls me, in so many ways, into a learning journey that weaves seamlessly into my real life.

At Willowstone Academy, we start with the transformative belief that we are partners with parents; it is a crucial pillar of our Learn Forward philosophy. This belief spurs us to link arms with parents in a transparent and consistent way to "learn" together how to best unlock student potential. We use the metaphor of the Table of Learning, a place where we all sit to learn: teacher, parent, student. Learning is central, even for the parents.

This culture within our learning community helps parents shed the often overwhelming pressure of having all the answers and instead, settle into the role of "learner" with their child and teacher. It also disrupts the traditional blame game schools and parents often play with each other regarding student progress and learning.

In order to set the tone, we set a theme each year that grounds our community in a learning journey. As an example, this year we chose the word "Rooted." Our professional graphic designer helps bring the theme to life within our Learn Forward philosophy, so social media and blogs can reinforce the stories of what is at the "roots" of our learning community. Then, throughout the year, we host equipping events for parents with refreshments, childcare, and high-value content on topics such as:

- Becoming technology savvy parents
- Cultivating adaptability in this age of acceleration
- The body science of healthy conversations about sexuality
- Managing mental health issues through mindfulness

In practical terms, we use a myriad of strategies to cultivate authentic and focused relationships with parents for the purpose of championing the extraordinary learning potential of every child. Amongst traditional tactics like email, report cards, and student-led conferences, we use the online tool FreshGrade to create digital, real-time portfolios with rich evidence of learning. We can only change the learning journey if we change assessment.

Each FreshGrade post and portfolio empowers parents to have reflective conversations with students. When learning conversations happen regularly within a supportive environment, learners cultivate improved self-awareness, envision and set their own learning goals, and monitor progress more effectively. Parents can offer support and accountability naturally at the dinner table or at bedtime because the learning experience was opened up through an image, video, or description of the learning happening at school.

Parents are deeply committed to championing the extraordinary potential in their child and have unrealized capacity to support a path of personalized learning. As educators, we can design cultures and processes to support a student's growth in the necessary competencies for the future. Our clear purpose is to re-imagine the essential relationships required to effectively champion a child's extraordinary potential and thereby maximize the education revolution of our time.

If you want to learn more, please check out the Table of Learning theme on the Learn Forward blog (www.learforward.ca). Additionally, in Bryan Goodwin's article "Research Matters - The Power of Parental Expectations," I love the section called *Distilling the "Magic" of Parent Support.* Research discovered that homes cultivating a learner's habit of mind or a culture of growth may be more effective than more traditional parent activities,

> *We might reconsider, however, what's really happening in home environments that support student success. Perhaps students in such homes aren't being forced into compliance-oriented behaviors like doing homework, but rather, developing an internal desire to work hard, persist, and succeed academically.*
>
> (Educational Leadership, September 2017, Volume 75)

So, I encourage every school leader to freely use the Table of Learning metaphor. Encourage everyone within the community to position themselves as learners and for all of us to cultivate a *Learn Forward* attitude as we journey together! Let me know how it goes via Twitter or Instagram @Learn_Forward!

Want to Know More?

Who to Follow:
Twitter:
@WillowstoneAcad
@MrsDrapersClass
@NeufeldInst
@SearchInstitute
@KeepConnectedSI
@CourageandRenewal

Additional Resources:
http://learnforward.ca/

Leading with Families

Amber Teamann @8amber8, Principal, Whitt Elementary, Wylie ISD

Whitt Elementary is in a close knit, higher socio-economic part of Wylie ISD. Our campus had an active, extremely active, and involved parent base. I knew immediately upon being named principal that I needed them on my side and that together we would continue to do incredible things. One of the first steps was establishing a unifying hashtag. #WeAreWhitt was born through surveying the community for suggestions via social media and then asking our staff to vote on the one they felt would be a positive, inclusive message for our campus vision. I had parents who were extremely educated and not only wanted what was best for their student, but also had a pretty good idea of how that should happen. I knew I needed them to understand me, what I believed as an educator and leader, and what incredible things their Wolves were doing.

We all know that social media can be a blessing and a curse, but I chose to leverage the connection I could make to meet and get to know as many of the 662 families as I possibly could. When families or staff would "friend" me, I accepted. I am fortunate enough to be in a district that not only allows this connection, but also encourages it. I am friends with my principal peers, my superintendent, and my pastor. There's not a whole lot of inappropriate content or whining that goes on my page to begin with! I've heard that I should keep my personal and professional life separate, but let's be real. You can't work 50+ hours a week, have children in the community, or care as much as we do and not have those lines blurred. I wanted my parents and my staff to see me as Amber, a wife, a mom, a leader ... to get to see who I am as a whole person, not the stereotyped version of what a principal is in their head. Joe Sanfelippo and Tony Sinanis have a great line in *Hacking Leadership* that says in absence of knowing what you do, people make up what they think you do. I wanted to head that off as quick as I could!

Right when I began, I started a couple of initiatives that I thought would make a difference in connecting our families to our classrooms. I worked with our staff to all create closed, private Facebook pages of their classrooms. We wanted transparency all the way around. I began posting a LOT to our Facebook page, as the principal, just sharing out all the really great things I got to see their Wolves doing. I hosted a "Tea with Teamann" to get to know our PTA board. It was a get to know me and an opportunity for them to ask me any questions they might have. I've continued that tradition each year, always with snacks and am always open to hear any suggestions from the group. Postcards were another way I tried to build connections and relationships. Each year I send each Wolf a postcard, from me. I celebrate accomplishments I see on Facebook, I celebrate things their teachers share with me, or things that I come across as I am out and about in the building. These are a BIG DEAL to families and are so personal! Throughout the years, we've added several events that allow our parents to feel like they are a part of what #wearewhitt is all about. Announcements are delivered on Facebook Live, we have events like "chalk the walk," "popsicles with the principals," or bedtime read alouds (again, delivered via FB) all designed with the intent to make people feel as if they are a part of our team.

When people feel like they are a part of something bigger than they are, I've found that they are all in and willing to support you whenever or however they can. When you build connections, you make a difference. I am fortunate enough to have gotten to know and love a family whose three boys have all gone through Whitt. Their youngest, Levi, has Down Syndrome. His journey in public education has been a challenge and ultimate success, which has in turn made me a better person. I was fortunate enough to be nominated and named the Dallas Educator of the Year from the Down Syndrome Guild through my relationship with his family. While they think I've done something special to make him be as included and connected as he is, I know that he is a Wolf, and that all Wolves, all our students, deserve to be celebrated and loved, regardless of anything else.

Want to Know More?

Who to Follow on Instagram:
@MMiller7571
Melissa Kartimas @lilmeli22
Stephanie McConnell @principalprinciples Lindsy
   Stumpenhorst @principal_in_boots Principal
   Williams @Principal_Williams

Additional Resources:
www.amberteamann.com

Creating Conversations

Jay Posik @posickj, Merton Intermediate Principal, Merton Wisconsin.

Our biggest partner in our students' learning, both academic and behavioral, are families. What we do to reach out to families is vital to this success. There are a variety of ways to create, build, and foster these relationships. Some of them occur within schools, but there are also ways to connect outside of school.

Many of us have an Open House or Family Information Nights to start the school year. These are great opportunities to get to know families, their hopes and dreams for their children, and their interest in helping out at school. But this is a one and done opportunity. In my years of experience, I have found that there are many ways to continue these conversations.

Principal chats, sometimes sponsored by the PTO, provide an opportunity to share what's happening in school as well as a chance to discuss topics of interest such as curriculum or procedures in place to keep our learners safe. Attendance at PTO meetings, and being a part of the agenda, also provides an opportunity for principals to interact with families. There are other ways to connect with families that don't necessarily involve meetings. Introduce the band and choir before a concert and hang around afterwards to have discussions. Have a table at National Night Out and handout school swag to all who stop by. At conferences, be visible, have conversations with families waiting to see teachers, join in on conferences either to be a part of a celebration or as part of a plan for improvement, and never miss the chance to thank a family for attending.

In my opinion, the most important way to connect with families is conversations, either face to face or on the phone. Families want to know that we care about their children and what better way than having individual conversations. Unfortunately, most of these conversations occur because a learner is not doing well academically or behaviorally. But because of a friend in my PLN, Mark French, principal of Gatewood Elementary School in Minnetonka, Minnesota, I've begun to be more consistent with having conversations about the good a learner is doing at school – the #GoodNewsCallOfTheDay. You can follow the hashtag #GoodNewsCallOfTheDay on Twitter to see the power of these connections.

Not all families are able to come to school because of their work schedule, their dislike of school growing up, or their history of school for their own children. Because of this, we need to find other ways to share the great things that are happening in our schools. As Joe Sanfelippo, superintendent from Fall Creek Schools in Wisconsin, would say, "Never give up the opportunity to say something great about your school." We use Instagram (mertonint), Twitter (@merton-int), and Facebook (Merton Intermediate School) to share our school story with families and the world. Newsletters are great options to share your school's story with families that don't use social media. Online newsletters, like Smore, provide options to share information about the school, upcoming events, parenting thoughts, and pictures.

One of my favorite family engagement ideas happened when some families, teachers, and I had a book chat for *Beyond the Bake Sale*, a book with great ideas to improve family engagement and involvement in our schools. Our PTO provided the books for us and we met once a month from October to March. The conversations during these discussions were open and honest. Because of these conversations, we made changes to our Open House and provided more options for families to be involved in our school.

We have found if you have an idea, and ask for families to be involved, they will show up to help out. Our PTO asks for treats for the holidays, conferences, or staff appreciation days, and our families bring in more than what we even need. Career Day allows family members to share their careers with our students. During Career Day, some family members are also a part of our interview team, an opportunity for our learners to be a part of an actual interview.

Want to Know More?

Who to Follow:
Twitter:
Ted Huff @TedHiff
Joe Mazza @Joe_Mazza
Julie Pile @JuliePile
@KeepConnectedSI
@CourageandRenewal

Hashtags to Watch:
Parent Camp parentcamp.org
Search on Twitter: Beyond the Bake Sale

Takeaways for Tomorrow

Invite yourself in. Find a family that you want to get to know better and see if they would let you come over to their house to talk more about their own story and their hopes and dreams not only for their child, but for themselves.

Call them. Make a point to call five to ten parents each week to thank them for a specific reason that their child is a gift to your school. Bonus points if you can include the child on the conference call.

Attend an important event. It could be a cultural celebration, a birthday party, or a funeral. Step outside your own culture and comfort and walk into a new setting and situation that will build a solid foundation with families.

Reach back, reach forward. Before I make a parent call, I always review our student information system to look into the names, ages, and grades of other siblings. Usually I have had at least one other child either from my days at the middle/high school, or my recent years in the kindergarten center. Taking an extra moment to ask how a future/former child is doing also shows that you care about the family, not just a student in your school today.

Meet up with a former student. With social media, connecting with former students is a lot easier than before. I have met with many former students, now adults (and some even parents of students I will serve) and ask them to tell me about their experiences as a student in our school. Take note and invite them again. Having multiple voices at the table only proves to improve the school.

A Few Final Thoughts

Families are our students' first teachers. They set the foundation for learning, connections to their culture, and model the character that they hope their own children learn and lead from as children through adulthood. As leaders, it is essential we think of families as a first thought, not an afterthought. Spending time in their homes, in the community, and meeting with them well before, and sometime after their children are in our schools, will establish the value of their role in our schools and will certainly impact how you lead. With all these strategies, ideas, and unconventional ways to connect with the stakeholders directly connected to our school, the next chapter will provide a connection to those school leaders in other buildings and at the district level.

Social Media Mantra

- What if we invested time in our children, two to three years before they became our students? **#UnConLeader**
- Sometimes how you say it and how often makes more of a difference than anything else you do in the school year. **#UnConLeader**
- If I am afraid to visit their home ... how can I be a fearless leader and advocate for their success? **#UnConLeader**

Create your own! Use the hashtag #UnConLeader to share your own takeaways

CHALLENGE

AFTER READING THIS CHAPTER I AM INTRIGUED BY THIS TOPIC:

I WILL LEARN MORE BY FOLLOWING THESE #UnConLeaders:

TAKE A PICTURE OF YOUR LEARNING WORK IN ACTION!
USE THE HASHTAG SO WE CAN LEAD TOGETHER!

#UnConLeader

Want to Learn More?

Cabeen, J. (2018). *Hacking early learning*. Highland Heights, OH: Times 10.

Robinson, K. (2015). *Creative schools*. New York: Penguin Books.

Rush, M. (2018). *Beat boredom: Engaging tuned-out teenagers*. Portland, ME: Stenhouse Publisher.

4 Leading with Colleagues or Central Office Administrators

Too often stories and strategies of creative ways to engage and inspire school communities stop at the school setting. In this chapter we will look at the leaders outside of the school walls and find unconventional ways to highlight how they make a difference.

Sometimes school leaders forget that sharing your message needs to happen up the leadership chain, not just out to the public. Sharing your message includes finding ways to include the other administrators within the district in the conversation.

School leaders also need to build a network with other building principals and school leaders – we can't fully prepare our students for the next level of learning if we haven't even spent time in other schools' classrooms or have a strong sense of the culture and climate of the buildings above, below, and next to us in grade level bands.

Having the tough conversations doesn't always happen with those directly above or below you in leadership. We will also explore how to have the tough and necessary conversations and share examples of frameworks you can use to set a foundation of trust and open the door to creative risk-taking in your schools.

In this chapter we will look at ways to include other principals, central office administrators, and school board members in authentically being a part of your school's story.

THE FURTHER AWAY YOUR POSITION TAKES YOU FROM THE CLASSROOM

PROVIDES YOU MORE OPPORTUNITIES TO MAKE CREATIVE IMPACTS ON THE SCHOOLS AND COMMUNITY YOU SERVE.

#UNCONLEADER

Linking the Learning

The Building Blocks of a Team

Circling back to coaching, but on a larger scale this time. Supporting a team as the school leader is more clear cut than being a team member with other principals, central office staff, and additional leadership positions. Our roles and responsibilities may braid, but also blur with different voices and visions at the table. In order to create a system that has student success, safety, and engagement at its core, coherence and capacity building is key.

One key to this approach is to develop a common knowledge and skill base across all leaders and educators in the system, focusing on a few goals, and sustaining an intense effort over multiple years Fullan and Quinn 2016). Too often leaders get so caught up in the stuff that we forget the substance. This can have a ripple effect with our teachers as they are looking for a clear, stable vision and leader to lead, support, and champion their work. When initiatives come and go this trust is eroded and work starts to be less bold and more cautious, as teachers are worried – what more will come on my plate before something comes off. Leaders at all levels need to be conscious not about how much is on the plate, but why it is there and the importance and value of each piece to the whole.

As a leader in a school that fed into four different elementary schools, communication and clear vision was essential. While each school had a specific culture, a dedicated lens of learning, and educators that intricately crafted personalized lessons for their students – we had to agree on a key learning target so students had a more seamless transition. One of these goals was to align our reading curriculum K-4. This meant that as school leaders we had to communicate clear non-negotiables back to our own schools. What are the key concepts that all students should master by grade level and how will we determine what mastery looks like? What systems will we consistently use to benchmark students and monitor growth? How to we look at data and identify students who would benefit from enrichment and those that could utilize some remediation for success? Creating common frameworks and processes for these questions lessened the guessing game for educators and created a more seamless transition from grade to grade and building to building. These conversations were standard items on our Elementary Principal monthly agenda and throughout the years we made sure to invite other specialists to the table (English Language Learning Leadership, Special Education Leadership, and the Data Assessment Coordinator for example).

But without strong leadership above guiding building leaders towards a common destination, speed bumps, flat tires, and detours could have easily derailed the work. A strong central office team is the district backbone, leading all stakeholders to a common vision with a clearer view; a view that steps away from the buildings and a broader perspective that reaches the PreK-Career community.

Asking for Help

Please remember that you are not alone in this ever changing, ever challenging work. In a survey done by the National Association of Secondary School Principals (NASSP) and the American Association of School Administrators (AASA) (2017) 94% of school leaders agreed that additional professional development and training opportunities would be helpful in their role, 81% agreed training in executive leadership would be useful, and only a little more than half felt supported by their district through professional learning opportunities.

Where do you go to find these supports? In Minnesota principals have been fortunate to apply to the Minnesota Principal Academy, a collaboration with the Minnesota Department of Education, Minnesota Elementary School Principals' Association, the Minnesota Association of Secondary School Principals, and the University of Minnesota. Housed at the University of Minnesota, principal cohorts meet for two days, 16 times, over the course of 18 months. Units of study are grounded in the National Institute of School Leadership (NISL) and facilitated by practicing principals, superintendents, curriculum directors, and other Minnesota leaders. The results – graduates feel supported in the work they are to do, they have time to read and review quality research, and have a space in which to debate the application with other school leaders across the state.

Are you a part of your state and national principal organizations? Both NASSP and NAESP have top notch annual conferences, webinars, monthly journals/newsletters, and an ever-growing presence on social media that supports school leaders in navigating this tremendously important work.

Now that you have some ideas of where to go – it is time to ask. In small rural communities I have seen K-12 principals save all their money to attend the state leadership conference and year after year say it is an investment well spent. Other leaders in larger districts create a rotation so every principal within the unit has an opportunity to attend a conference or professional development at least once every two to three years. Some districts have staff development funds that are readily accessible by school leaders; other buildings set aside some of their building dollars for their school leaders to receive ongoing training.

The Barrier: The Leader

Too often I have sat next to someone in one of these workshops, conferences, or symposiums that are just there to collect their CEUs. Or the ones who come back and complain about the traffic, the lines at registration, or the time spent away from their golf game more than the learning they could have brought back and shared with others. While we work to find just in time and just right PD for our teachers, too often we neglect our own needs, and at a detriment to those we serve.

The challenge: take the risk. Leaders are always learning. If this is something you believe, then it is something your school needs to see in action.

- Share the learning. In your weekly staff memo, attach an article or summarize a book you are reading.
- Phone a friend. Bring a principal intern along to a state workshop, legal seminar, or other learning opportunity.
- Connect at the state level. Your leadership organizations will never turn away a member willing to roll up their sleeves and join in the work of educating, advocating, and supporting schools.
- Include your boss. Make sure to loop in your supervisor in anything you are attending, wanting to participate in, or interested in pursuing. Remember that study of Principals and District Leaders earlier on? 90% of the district leaders thought that additional professional development and training opportunities would be helpful to their school leaders and 80% of superintendents agreed or *strongly agreed* that executive leadership training was an area where their school leaders could use more support.

Watch Out for Speedbumps, Detours, and Texting While Driving to the Destination

You have a plan, you did your research, you created leadership teams to pilot the project, students have buy in, families are excited, but you forgot to loop in the leaders around and above you and shortly you find out that your project has stalled, or stopped. At times as school leaders we get so caught up in the day to day operations of our school we forget about maintaining connections with those whose view is a few thousand feet higher than yours and integrating that voice in the decisions you are making. Communicating the concerns, conflicts, and celebrations are critical for the growth of the organization, and the support you need for your school.

- **Set up monthly meetings**. Find a time to connect with your supervisor on a monthly basis and create an agenda to go through. Grows and glows, personal goals, site-based goals, and data to support where you are in this process is incredibly important. Ask them what information you are missing or what implication this work will have on the schools above and below you. The more frontloading you do with your work, the more support and the better the end result will be.

- **Stay focused**. Be careful not to make this a competition. Just because the other middle school in town is moving to a block schedule, doesn't mean you should as well. Pick one thing and do it well before you move onto the next. If you are focused on reviewing your Grading Practices, it is okay to say not right now to a district initiative to implement healthy snacks during the school day. If something comes across your desk as an ask, not a mandate, find a way to communicate that you see value in this idea, but that right now your team is moving in a direction in which this doesn't seem to fit.

- **Don't multitask in meetings**. In administrative meetings, does your computer come up when an agenda item that doesn't pertain to you and your school? Challenge yourself to stay engaged – even if it is a topic way outside your own context. By leaning in and listening to other agenda items with intent you might find an unconventional way to fund your new outdoor classroom, update the cameras in your school, or find a place that will provide your materials and set up your Holiday Hot Chocolate Bar for staff without you having to go out and do it yourself.

- **Ask for help**. This winter my former direct supervision was stuck outside, in the cold, with me for an hour guiding traffic at our high school. I took this opportunity as a way to ask a question about my own leadership and a recent plan that went off course. Because of his higher view of the organization, and his knowledge of my leadership style (ten years and counting of working together), he was able to identify the missteps and found ways to move forward that I couldn't see for myself.

- **Poke holes in my idea.** Have an idea of a new master schedule, implementing PLCs, changing the elective offerings, or integrating 1:1 in a more student driven way? A strategy I use is to ask stakeholders to come in and "poke holes in my ideas." While this is a way to see from other viewpoints, as the initiator of the ideas it is essential to walk into this think-tank with an open mind, and leave your defensive responses at the door.

A STRONG CENTRAL OFFICE TEAM IS BEHIND THE SCENES

DOING THE HEAVY LIFTING SO SCHOOL LEADERS CAN TRY NEW THINGS.

#UNCONLEADER

#UnConLeader Twitter Connections

People to Follow:
Jeff Zoul @Jeff_Zoul
http://jeffreyzoul.blogspot.com/
Tony Sinanis @TonySinanis
http://leadingmotivatedlearners.blogspot.
   com/
Joe Sanfelippo @Joe_Sanfelippo
www.jsanfelippo.com/
   leadership-challenge
Starr Sackstein @mssackstein
www.mssackstein.com/
Winston Sakurai @winstonsakurai
The School Superintendents Association
   @AASAHQ
www.aasa.org/home/

Hashtags to Watch:
#1minwalk2work
#engagechat
#SuptChat
#PrinLeaderChat
#BookCampPD

Other Places to Check Out:
Minnesota Principal Academy:
   http://innovation.umn.edu/mnpa/
National Institute for School Leaders:
   www.nisl.org/
John Maxwell: www.johnmaxwell.com/

#UnConLeader Keys

Who do you go to when you have a question? Find your tribe and set dedicated
   time to problem solve, process, and create systems for supports for each of
   your sites.

How are you sharing and celebrating with your colleagues?

Innovation, Growth Mindset, and Fear-Based Responses

Muhammed (2018) states this so well: "Innovation has a fighting chance if
it is being implemented within a healthy, human environment." Creating
that healthy, human environment is essential for any next step your school
or district is planning on taking. This next narrative could have taken a
wrong turn right away. Sitting in an administrative meeting, gearing up for
the next school year and the Director of Educational Services unveiled
the Principal Professional Development for the next year: Brave New
Workshop.

Yes, as a district our leadership would have a yearlong dive into the
process of risk taking and innovation driven by a comedy improvisation
club. Initially I was grounded in the middle school girl mentality that drives

me crazy on the other side of leadership. Why in the world would we do such a thing? How in the world is this going to help us grow as a team, and more importantly how is this going to improve my abilities to lead a major technology integration plan at the Kindergarten Center? Feet dragging (and internal eye rolling), I walked into the first workshop. Margi Simmons, the Director of Applied Improvisation at BNW (Brave New Workshop), was standing there smiling with a colleague and within in minutes we started improvisational activities.

These activities ranged from thinking and saying whatever came to your mind immediately, role playing unrealistic and silly scenarios, and working through some reframing exercises. Grounded in this work is their Big Five (Sweeney 2016):

- Listen: be present, open and aware
- Defer judgment: pause and accept the potential of ideas and opinions
- Reframe: use what you have to move forward
- Declare: be authentic and clear, speak your mind
- Jump in: develop a bias towards action, avoid analysis paralysis

A few sessions in, I was drinking the juice. I learned through awkward activities that I tended to put up defensive fear-based behaviors when I was scared of sounding "stupid." I didn't offer ideas that I hadn't vetted 100 times over in my head, and wow, if someone else suggested something I didn't agree with – well, I would put up my own form of a wall. Through this process I really dug into my own behaviors and how they were disrupting the leadership team from growing, and in the process myself. But the true test was, how could this translate into the technology initiative back at the Kindergarten Center? An initiative that was critical to get right, right away. An initiative that involved 70% of a staff that didn't experience this form of technology in their education and now was responsible for teaching and learning at the same time, and sometimes at a slower pace than their five-year-old students?

Sitting down with the Director that brought in Brave New Workshop, we mapped out activities that would address the most common fear-based behaviors that would come up during the trainings and deployed them during the half-day workshops. He found ways to gamify the professional development as he knew these teachers very well, and appreciated the importance of play in our school day and suggested it be a part of our professional learning as well. He supported and assisted in finding funding to purchase "prizes" such as apps, Lego kits, robots, and coding games for teachers to check out and use within their classes – no strings attached. He coordinated a day for the Technology Director and me to go the SMART-Board headquarters and meet with Zack Krueger, an incredible educator and trainer for our school in the implementation of this work. And most importantly, he showed up for each of these professional development days, participated in the activities, and came back during the instructional day to see the work in action and support the educators in the work.

We played a game of "What's in the box" – an activity in which someone gives you a "gift" and you have to respond with gratitude for that gift and one way in which you would use it in a positive way. Examples ranged from a class full of head lice, 7th day in a row of indoor recess, and all of your iPads simultaneously updating – right before you released the class to independent work. Right after that activity which left most people in tears – from laughter – we transitioned into the workshop in which teachers learned to create their own SMART-lessons that were derived from Academic Standards, and allowed students to create their own responses vs consuming a purchased app from the iPad. At the end of the session we watched teams of educators get up on "stage" and show off their learning – fear aside. The follow up from that work included going in and observing the work in action, the excitement of the students, and the pride from the teachers accomplishing something they never even thought they would need to try.

At the beginning of this story, I wasn't able to see the connection between improv and improving the learning for students and staff. For someone who values the unconventional nature of elevating learning, this idea was a little too farfetched for even me! However, three years later I look back at that year as one of incredible growth and learning that I take with me intentionally in so much of what I do on a daily basis. You know the saying "what would you do if you knew you couldn't fail?" Through this journey I learned the important lessons of what you can learn when you do fail, fall, take risks, and try all over again.

#UnConLeader Twitter Connections

People to Follow:
George Couros @gcouros
Websites:
The Principal of Change: https://georgecouros.
  ca/blog/
Eric Sheninger @E_Sheninger
http://esheninger.blogspot.com/
Jon Gordon @JonGordon11
www.jongordon.com/
Chip Baker @ChipBakerTSC
Podcast: The Success Chronicles
Kristan Rodriguez @Dr_Rodriguez21
Glenn Robbins @Glennr1809
Neil Gupta @drneilgupta_
Blog: https://drneilgupta.wordpress.com/
Glenn Robbins @Glennr1809_

Hashtags to Watch:
#InnovatorsMindset
Other Places to Check Out:
Visible Learning @VisibleLearning
www.visiblelearningplus.com/
William D. Parker:
  www.williamdparker.com/
The Schoolhouse 302:
  https://theschoolhouse302.com/

#UnConLeader Keys
Try to "yes … and" an idea from another staff member this week.
Get in the habit of practicing growth mindsets when you are most afraid.

Leaders in the Field

Leaping into New Leadership

Suzanne Mitchell, Administrative Officer, @suzannereads

So, what happens when you love being a principal and you are asked to consider taking your influence to the next level? To leave your school, your teachers, your kids? Frankly, my initial reaction was a loud and resounding no. Never. Not happening. Not me. District leadership was not in my five-year plan. Or my ten-year plan. Being a principal was the best job in the world! I was content … wasn't I?

Then our superintendent pointed out how many of our 46 principals had less than three years of experience and our deputy superintendent shared his belief that principal coaches would be valuable. And they wanted me to do it. I admit I was intrigued. As a principal, I often wished I had a coach, but could I *be* one? Mel Robbins' book, *The 5 Second Rule*, speaks to how quickly your mind can become a saboteur by flooding your thoughts with doubts. Within seconds of seriously considering the offer, questions began racing through my mind. Could I really make a difference? Could I fill our leader mentorship gap? Could I provide a safe relationship for leaders to talk through decisions that were weighty; without judgement or evaluative repercussions? Could I learn to ask the right questions? Questions that helped principals discover their own solutions or provide insight to their very real dilemmas? Would they expect me to have all the right answers? Know every state and board policy by heart? Was I capable enough, respected enough, wise enough? With all that swirling in my head, I said yes anyway. While I knew there would be doubts, uncertainty, and setbacks I believed in our principals and the power in their roles as difference makers for students.

Six months into the role, some principals have embraced the concept and welcomed my colleague and me into their school family. Others are more independent or hesitant, and I understand. Trust takes time. Through it all, the foundational questions that ground the work have been "What did I need as a principal? What kind of support grows, enhances, and builds capacity?" We shifted the format of the new principal meetings in order to assist first-year principals in processing the mountain of information they received from the monthly district meeting. A Google doc is shared with new principals to insert questions/comments as they are in the district meeting. We order lunch for first-year principals and meet immediately after the larger meeting, so we can clarify expectations, guide discussions, and answer questions as principals determine which items presented need immediate attention, which can wait, and when they should delegate. We celebrate wins and affirm progress, no matter how small, and we offer feedback when things do not go as planned.

In early December, we hosted our first principal retreat. Even though it was December and optional, we had eleven of our 46 principals attend. Extended conversations were facilitated around student data, improving PLCs, school culture, and staff morale, all of which were topics selected by attendees in an EdCamp style format. All who attended have asked for a spring retreat and have committed to bringing another principal along. Between meetings, we serve as thought partners for everything from discipline decisions to how to handle the team that does not work well together. Our goal is to listen and ask questions to help principals think through and make the best decisions for their school and stakeholders.

Was the leap in this new level of leadership worth it? Absolutely. Do I still have a lot to learn? Without a doubt. But each time a principal says, "thanks for thinking that through with me" or "that's a great question, I hadn't thought about it like that," I know I made the right leap.

Want to Know More?

Who to Follow:
Twitter:
@SteeleThoughts
@RLGMike Author of *The Artisan Teacher* and founder of Rutherford Learning Group

Additional Resources:
Podcasts:
Nobody does principal support better than these guys:
Better Leaders Better Schools with Daniel Bauer
Transformative Principal with Jethro Jones

Transformational Leadership

Dr. Steven Weber is the Associate Superintendent with Fayetteville Public Schools (Arkansas). Connect with Weber on Twitter at @curriculumblog

In my early years as a curriculum director, I saw my role as a problem solver. When teachers and administrators had a question, it was my role to read an education book, develop professional development, and lead the way. Seeing yourself as a superhero responding to the Bat Signal is one way to view the role of a leader. However, you can only solve so many problems before teachers and administrators realize that you cannot possibly have the answer to every question.

Since 2000, I have studied leadership, worked with teacher leaders, attended conferences, observed in classrooms, and asked educators more about their role in K-12 education. These are some of the leadership lessons learned from over the past decade. Leading with questions, rather than solving problems, has provided me with multiple perspectives and I have grown as a leader by participating in Edcamps, Twitter Chats, Voxer Groups, and through focusing on Leadership Development.

Edcamps: Leave Your Title at the Door

When you enter an Edcamp, you leave your title at the door. It doesn't matter if you are a superintendent, department chair, counselor, assistant principal, or curriculum coordinator. Once you enter an Edcamp, you are a connected educator, leader, learner, collaborator, and friend. As a leader, I enjoy hearing multiple perspectives. Some meetings I attend are for principals only or central office staff only. Edcamps allow me to listen to the perspectives of a first-year teacher, a department chair, a superintendent, a second-year assistant principal, a state teacher of the year, a media specialist, a university professor, and a director of professional development. There are leaders at every level in a school district and Edcamp(s) remind me of the power of providing each person with a voice and leadership opportunities.

Twitter Chats and Voxer Groups: Continuous Improvement

When I entered the field of education, I remember the excitement when a professional journal would arrive in my mailbox. Once a month, I would have the opportunity to connect with authors, educators, and university professors who were writing about K-12 education and research. Over the past ten years, I have enjoyed participating in Twitter Chats where educators share their perspectives, highlight instructional strategies from their classroom, and share resources to support teaching and learning. Early in my career, becoming a connected educator meant attending the annual state conference. Social media has provided opportunities for me to connect with educators who impact my leadership and who transform teaching and learning in our school district through their blogs, resources, and podcasts.

Voxer Groups are similar to Twitter Chats, but they involve text and voice. At any point in the week, I can learn from educators from Los Angeles to Baltimore. Voxer Groups may involve teacher leaders, assistant principals, principals, curriculum directors, and superintendents. These groups share what they are learning, and I am able to share their resources with teachers and administrators in our school district. I still look forward to receiving education journals in the mail, but my leadership would not be the same if I did not connect with other educators through Twitter Chats and Voxer Groups.

Multiplying Leaders: Give Others a Platform

District leaders often fall into the trap of feeling like their job is to have all the answers. There is no such thing as a perfect leader and great leaders provide others with leadership opportunities. Teacher leaders can provide instructional leadership, data analysis, curriculum development, program review, and professional development. Great district leaders focus on adding value to others and providing leadership opportunities. Multiplying leaders can include a mentoring program, book study, Voxer Group, aspiring leaders program, or taking a group of leaders to a conference.

Leadership: It's a Journey You Take with Others

Do you remember the first time a principal or district leader sent you to a professional conference? Do you recall the first time you were asked to serve on a district committee? This may have been the moment you saw yourself as a leader. The role of a district leader is to invest in others. Developing the leaders around you requires an outward focus rather than an inward focus. As you grow as a leader, you will begin to see that transformational leadership is a journey that you take with other educators!

Five Questions For Transformational Leaders

1. Who invested in me?
2. What are my strengths as an educator?
3. Whom can I invest in and support?
4. How will listening to multiple perspectives help me grow as a leader?
5. How will our school or school district benefit from multiple leaders?

Want to Know More?

Who to Follow:
@Rosalsiah
@RossCoops31
@drneilgupta
@cjakicic
@DCulberhouse

Additional Resources:
The Power of Moments
The Third Teacher:
http://thethirdteacherplus.com/resources
Learning Personalized:
www.learningpersonalized.com/
Good Leaders Ask Great Questions
Cult of Pedagogy:
www.cultofpedagogy.com/

Takeaways for Tomorrow

Give a compliment. So often we read the importance of recognizing our students and staff – but what about our colleagues, in other buildings and central office. Set aside a few minutes every month (or week) to send a note, make a call, or connect with one of these key members of the organization and thank them for the work they do every day to support the schools they serve.

Invite them in. Do you have a concert, an incentive, a shortened day? Invite your supervisors in to help. Central Office staff came from the classroom and those gifts they had then can be used now – all you have to do is ask.

What is your vision? Kotter (2012) reminds us that whenever you can't describe the vision or change initiative in five minutes or less and get a reaction that signifies both understanding and interest – you are in for trouble. When rolling out a plan, vet it with key people to make sure your message is clear, succinct, and everyone can see themselves in the work.

Create a one-pager. Along with Kotter's work, I am a huge fan of one-pagers. Whatever you are implementing make sure you have an elevator speech and one-pager to support the work. When creating these plans also share with your leadership and your peers. Why reinvent a wheel when you are surrounded with other leaders that can build upon the greatness you are creating to make it even better?

Make every meeting meaningful. Stop meeting just to meet. Seriously. Think ahead of the big dates, big initiatives, and bring together teams to help create activities and agendas that engage staff in the work, not just sit and get. Or better yet flip your meetings – use a Friday Focus for the nuts and bolts and use meeting time to break into small groups and have deeper discussions around the core topics at the time.

A Few Final Thoughts

All leaders are leaders, and we can learn so much from each other. Unconventional leadership means taking a look at what other leaders are doing, no matter what the context or setting, and learn from them. Lead like a learner, take risks, fall forward, and have fun in the process. Take intentional time to connect and find ways to celebrate each other's success, share resources, and create a strong safety net of supports for all stakeholders. Creating spaces to invite our other leaders in and going out is essential to bridging these worlds together. Next, we look at extending our net a little further by connecting with community agencies, employers, and legislative stakeholders.

Social Media Mantra

- The further away your position takes you from the classroom provides you more opportunities to make creative impacts on the schools and community you serve. **#UnConLeader**
- A strong central office team is behind the scenes doing the heavy lifting so school leaders can try new things. **#UnConLeader**

Create your own! Use the hashtag #UnConLeader to share your own takeaways.

CHALLENGE

AFTER READING THIS CHAPTER I AM INTRIGUED BY THIS TOPIC:

I WILL LEARN MORE BY FOLLOWING THESE #UnConLeaders:

TAKE A PICTURE OF YOUR LEARNING WORK IN ACTION!
USE THE HASHTAG SO WE CAN LEAD TOGETHER!

Want to Learn More?

Fullan, M., & Quinn, J. (2016). *Coherence*. Thousand Oaks, CA: Corwin.

Kotter, J. (2012). *Leading change*. Boston, MA: Harvard Business Review Press.

Muhammad, A. (2018). *Transforming school culture*. Bloomington, IN: Solution Tree Press.

National Association of Secondary School Principals (2017). The changing the role of the school leader. Retrieved from www.principalsmonth.org/mckinsey/wp-content/uploads/2016/06/17_PD_McKinseyReport_P3D_web.pdf. Accessed on February 15, 2019.

Sweeny, J. (2016). *Innovative mindset*. Hoboken, NJ: Wiley.

5 Leading with Community Members or Legislative Stakeholders

Schools today need to become hubs of learning for the students we will serve tomorrow. As leaders we can no longer be passive in sharing our concerns and school celebrations with those outside of the system that can help us make the changes necessary for our students to thrive.

What do community members and legislative stakeholders need to know? School leaders matter. In a joint NAESP/NASSP publication (2013) the connection between investing in school leaders and the impact it has on student outcomes is evident. The new understanding of the principal's impact on learning should motivate all policymakers and others with a stake in student learning to advocate for effective, ongoing principal development.

As leaders it is on us to make our voices heard, and with social media, making connections with those partners is easier than ever. Sharing your school story and inviting partners into the work benefits everyone at the table. Understanding policy and platforms that support your school's mission and state priorities is essential to understand and advocate for the students and families you serve.

As Loria (2018) states, "There's tremendous power in establishing partnerships between schools and local community organizations, especially with nonprofit or mission-driven organizations." Developing that power and creating intentional connections that have sustained benefit for all parties in the partnership is essential for long-term success.

Unconventional partnerships with our community and our legislators is an opportunity to implement and sustain relationships with those outside of our school organization. The possibilities of partnerships are endless, however, unless we ask it won't happen. We don't know what they have to offer if we don't ask.

In this chapter we will look at the importance of having an understanding of communicating with legislators and other stakeholders in meaningful and timely ways. We will look at the importance of visible leadership within the community and the role and responsibilities we have to serve our students during the instructional day as well as becoming a voice for them in the community in which they live.

LIVING AND LEADING
WITHIN THE COMMUNITY
YOU SERVE REACHES
FAR BEYOND
THE TITLE ON YOUR
BUSINESS CARD

IT BECOMES WHO YOU ARE.

#UNCONLEADER

Linking the Learning

Unconventional Ways to Seek Incredible Partnerships

Have you ever asked someone to the prom? No seriously. While I may not have had the courage to ask someone while in high school, I have developed the confidence, vision, and passion to start asking now. Going out of your comfort zone, seeking partnerships that have never been considered, and not taking no for an answer, parallels the nervousness and fear of asking someone out to the big event. I have been known to be a little bit of a relentless leader when it comes to getting not what I wish for, but what our school really needs. In the pursuit of these needs I have found that asking for help, and asking again, is a recipe for success.

In Austin, Minnesota we are known for many things, and SPAM is just one of them. As the corporate headquarters of Hormel and the home of the SPAM brand museum there are many opportunities for partnerships with the schools. The Austin schools have benefitted from many generous donations from this company that has greatly enhanced our programming. But this time I had a big idea ... one that didn't require money, but time.

As an educator in the Saint Paul Public Schools I was able to participate in a program called *Everybody Wins MN!* With this literacy initiative, corporate volunteers would come into our school once a week and read with a "buddy" throughout the school year. After moving to Austin, and becoming the principal of the kindergarten center, this program seemed like a perfect fit for our school and community. The first ask was contacting the Minnesota headquarters of *Everybody Wins* to see if we could be accepted. Initially it was a no – we were rural, not diverse enough, and they didn't think we had the capacity of corporate volunteers to make this work. After a few conference calls, and an overview of this incredible community (at the time our school represented over 24 different home languages!), they said yes.

The second ask was to Hormel. A meeting was scheduled with the Director of Organizational Development at Hormel's world headquarters. I arrived armed with my data and ready to advocate for our students and this opportunity. Five minutes into the conference call between Hormel and *Everybody Wins* the deal was done! A month later 60 corporate volunteers filled an auditorium at Hormel and went through the process of becoming a trained volunteer. Two weeks later these volunteers jumped on two school buses and rode over to Woodson where they met their "buddy" and for the next eight weeks spent thirty minutes with them, reading to them, building relationships with them, and showing each student that their success in life could be influenced by community members that cared for them (Austin Daily Herald 2017).

People to Follow:
Deb Delisle @DebDelisle
Dr. Rosa Perez-Isiah @RosaIsiah
Website: http://rosaisiah.blogspot.com/
Amy Fast, EdD. @fastcrayon
Future Ready @FutureReady https://futureready.org/
New America @NewAmerica www.newamerica.org/
    education-policy/
Strive Together @StriveTogether
www.strivetogether.org/
Ed Review: www2.ed.gov/news/newsletters/edreview/index.html

Hashtags to Watch:
#WeLeadED
#WholeChild

#UnConLeader Keys
Find a community partner – invite them in – and start a conversation of how you
    can work together to enhance student success.

WHAT YOU POST

IS HOW YOU SHOW OTHERS WHAT IS IMPORTANT.

#UnConLeader

Social Media Rock Star

I am the first to admit, including social media into my daily leadership responsibilities was something I initially resisted. At the time there were more cautionary tales of putting yourself and your school out on the web than success stories. But after nudges from my PLN and seeing successful examples from other schools we set out to create our Facebook page and blog. At first it was a slow start, a picture here, a blog post there. Not a lot of systematic thought behind the timing or the posts – just a goal to put five pictures out a week and one post a month. While our start was slow on our end, our parents jumped on board right away. The likes, the tags, the follows grew – and not just for the year we were in our school. Parents still hop on the page years after their child graduated kindergarten to make a comment, congratulate a staff member, or reminisce about special holiday events. Once we started Facebook Live videos of our special events and concerts, that is when the grandparents jumped in. My last year at the kindergarten center I received three different thank you cards – from the same grandparent. She was a secretary at a school in another state and continued to share her gratitude for what we posted and how often she could see her grandchild engaged, and excited about learning.

Communicating the vision of your school isn't just about a one-pager, or a nicely displaced mission statement in your school office. Using social media shows community members and other stakeholders what you value and how you are cultivating and supporting students on a daily basis to become the successful adults everyone wants them to become.

Ask, ask, and ask again.

As a relentless advocate for your school's success, at times you will put yourself in environments that are completely out of your own realm and comfort zone, for me this is with the legislative and political components of leadership. While I have a sense why it is important to send a message to the legislators, I didn't have a clue how to do it. For years I paid my membership dues to our elementary principal association, but I didn't actively use the resources they provided. Once I started working with our state education department in creating a PreK-3 Leadership Series for our state that all changed.

In working with the Minnesota Elementary Principal Association, I learned our platforms, positions, and how to engage with my local officials. By reading the e-updates I saw other principals lobbying on the state and national capital and learned from them not only the importance of advocating for our schools, but the most impactful ways to do the work. I continued to offer to help with any advocacy, specifically with state initiatives supporting voluntary PreK across the state of Minnesota. I offered legislators tours of our school, I wrote articles for large newspapers and attended events that included state officials in government.

In March of 2017 the Executive Director of our state principal association called me. Governor Dayton is having a press release for funding for voluntary PreK and they ask for a principal to stand and speak next to him – you ready? While every part of my body was saying no, my heart and mouth said yes. Two days later, and hundreds of practices of my statement, I drove to Saint Paul, Minnesota and made my way through the capitol and into the Governor's private office. I might still have the napkin from the under the glass of water I had while talking with him after the press conference and our Lt. Governor about the day to day impact PreK has on our school and community. I walked into the capitol that day shaking and scared, I walked out excited and honored to have played a small part in supporting our state initiatives in education.

Getting ahead of the game.

I will be honest. For a few years when the weekly legislative update came from our state association legal and legislative counsel, Roger Aronson and I didn't pay much attention. At the time I was an assistant principal and I was so caught up in the day to day school operations I couldn't see the value of looking at the big picture, or what could be coming our way. Today, I am better than I was before, but still learning how to intentionally increase my voice at the legislative table. Now this doesn't mean I have to camp out at the state capitol but in each state, there are different ways to get involved, and some ways are not exclusive to you.

1. **Subscribe to legislative updates**. Each state has ways to get alerts and updates on programs and departments that are of interest to you. Currently I receive email updates on the K12 Science standard updates, special education finance, and anything involving licensure and administration.

2. **Share with staff.** This is modeled well by our Superintendent. He forwards weekly updates from a few different organizations: The Schools for Equity in Education, Minnesota School Board Association, Ed Review, and the Minnesota Department of Education weekly briefings for Superintendents.

3. **Give input.** Take the survey, give your feedback. Many times, state and national agencies want your voice via a survey or webinar. If it is a passion of yours, or it will impact your school share your voice, or better yet, include relevant staff in the process. In current Science Standard revisions, we have sent three teachers to workshops and webinars to get the most recent information to come back and share with our staff and the district office so we can prepare and plan for changes to be implemented within the next five years.

Your Voice Matters

As a leader people will believe what you say, so make sure you are saying it correctly. Recently I was out to dinner with my spouse and another couple at our table started asking questions on a pending school referendum. Now while the project has no direct ties to the middle school, I have a responsibility to provide community members (and voters) accurate information, and to withhold my own judgment. Had I responded with "I don't know anything about it," what is the unintentional message I am sending? Becoming a strong voice for our school community also means understanding the basic processes for local voting and what voters are voting on. In our district all administrators are briefed on referendums and have an opportunity to ask questions to ensure we have a consistent understanding and message for the community, and we all feel equipped to answer the questions that come our way. As our school is a polling place for our city, we have another opportunity to put our school and student's best foot forward. I love connecting with community members and enjoy the brief interactions they have with our students when they are in the building. It is really enjoyable to talk with our retired community members and to hear their recollection of what the building used to look like and their memories of middle school compared to our student's today. Even when the intention of coming into the school has nothing to do with our students, we are creating intentional interactions that when they leave they have had a positive experience with our stakeholders and have experienced the benefits of quality programming in our local community first hand.

#UnConLeader Twitter Connections

People to Follow:

NAESP @NAESP

www.naesp.org/advocacy

NASSP @NASSP

www.nassp.org/policy-advocacy-center/

America for Early Ed @SupportEarlyEd

http://americaforearlyed.org/

US Department of Education @usedgov

www.ed.gov/

National Education Association:
   @NEAToday www.nea.org/

EdWeek: www.edweek.org/ew/index.html

Hashtags to Watch:

#PrincipalsAdvocate

#PrinLeaderChat

State Chats:

#MNLEAD

#IAChat

#KSedchat

#VAESPChat

#OHEdChat

#NYEDChat

Other places to check out:

NAESP Advocacy Podcast: www.naesp.
   org/advocacy-podcasts

Woodson Kindergarten Center:
   www.facebook.com/
      WoodsonKindergartenCenter/

https://packersintraining.wordpress.com/

#UnConLeader Keys

Start following other schools on social media for ideas and ways to start sharing
   your own message on social media platforms.

Leaders in the Field

How do we support the Whole Educator?

Dr. Forrest Griek @FMGriek, Director of Labor Relations & Whole Educator Support, Tacoma Public Schools

Each morning, my own kids enter the gates of their elementary school and they are greeted with three prominent phrases painted on a cement wall outside their school: "Care for Yourself, Care for Each Other and Care for This Place." While at first glance you cannot help but want to embrace these words, you wonder if these words were part of a student art project that started and ended just as quickly as they were painted or if these words have life and a true context beyond that static wall. When you dig a little deeper you realize that "Care for Yourself, Care for Each Other and Care for This Place" is the school's mantra. Kids own these words and the staff have embraced the culture surrounding them. Even my kindergarten son has told his younger brother that, "we need to care for each other and care for this place."

I suspect that the school's mantra and its culture was spurred through Tacoma Public Schools' Whole Child Initiative, which has redefined how our schools addressed the social emotional needs of students. Prior to the inception of the Tacoma Whole Child Initiative in 2013 our students were struggling and we had a difficult time responding to their social emotional needs.

It has been five years since Tacoma Public Schools launched the Whole Child Initiative; we have been nationally recognized for this work and our kids are better supported. They are safer, healthier, better challenged, and more engaged. Today however, in the path of a national teacher shortage and a polarized society we are now asking, what about our educators? Do they feel supported? Are they safe? Are they healthy? Are they engaged?

In the last few years alone, the American Federation of Teachers (AFT) shared survey results of 5,000 educators. 61% reported that work is "always" or "often stressful" (Toppo 2017). The article went on to read that,

> More than half of the educators point out their mental health is an issue: 58% said their mental health was 'not good' for seven or more of the previous 30 days. A similar survey in 2015 found just 34% of respondents felt the same.

In addition to this trend of educator stress, our teachers are leaving the profession at an alarming rate. According to an article published by the Washington Post, (Strauss 2015), and research from Richard Ingersoll, a professor at the University of Pennsylvania, 40–50% of teachers leave the profession by the end of their fifth year.

It has become more apparent than ever that we need educators at the top of their game. The research suggests that our employees need more support. Furthermore, healthier employees equal better results. Dr. Anastasia Snelling from American University in D.C. and a leading expert on teacher health and wellness said, "A healthier teacher workforce translates into less absenteeism, higher retention rates, and improved productivity" (Snelling & Stevenson 2013).

Because of this need, TPS district level leadership began to ask questions. What does adult support look like in Tacoma Public Schools? How can we develop a system and a culture that responds to employee needs? One critical question though emerged at the top and ironically, it was the same question we were asking about our students five years go.

How do we support the Whole Educator? We began to rally. In our first attempt at answering this question, we launched the Whole Educator Initiative and essentially replicated the Whole Child tenets by focusing our support on employee health, safety, and engagement.

Tacoma Public Schools started this work by developing a one-stop internal website that allows TPS employees to access several resources to support them. These resources include health and wellness options, a variety of professional development opportunities, and community partner information to name a few. Over the last year, the Whole Educator Initiative has also been a staple at employee events across TPS. A Whole Educator Academy was held over the summer, drawing in more than 500 teachers to attend this two-day conference. Teachers could choose to attend a variety of sessions that supported their work in the classroom and beyond. Our second phase to this initiative included developing the metrics to measure employee safety, health, and engagement as well as encouraging employees to get active every day.

Most recently in our schools, some principals have taken on the Whole Educator Initiative and made it their own. Employees in these schools have reported being more energized and motivated to attend work each day. One specific example was a spin class at one of our comprehensive high schools. Spin class participants gather after school in the gym to spin. This activity inspired us to launch a 20 Minutes a Day campaign to promote wellness and encourage employees to get active. Some schools have created time in the main office to socialize and engage in collegial celebrations prior to the first bell.

While we have much more work to do around the Whole Educator Initiative to fully address the needs of all our employees, it is a start and we have begun to answer our original critical question: how do we support the Whole Educator? It is our belief that once each employee feels safe, healthy, and engaged they will truly thrive. In turn, so will the students we serve.

Want to Know More?

Who to Follow:

Twitter:

@ASCD

#WholeEducator

Tacoma Schools @tacomaschools

Washington State ASCD @WSASCD

Josh Garcia @Garciaj9Josh

Additional Resources:

www.washingtonpost.com/news/answer-sheet/wp/2017/12/20/educating-the-whole-child-isnt-just-jargon-heres-how-its-done/?noredirect=on&utm_term=.717435d6e412

www.tacomaschools.org/careers/Pages/whole-educator.aspx

Snelling, A. & Stevenson, M. (2013, March 10). Helping Teachers Get Healthier. Retrieved November 08, 2017, from www.edweek.org/ew/articles/2013/08/21/01snelling.h33.html

Strauss, V. (2015, June 12). Why so many teachers leave – and how to get them to stay. Retrieved November 08, 2017, from www.washingtonpost.com/news/answer-sheet/wp/2015/06/12/why-so-many-teachers-leave-andhow-to-get-them-to-stay/?utm_term=.b107097e6565

Toppo, G. (2017, October 30). Survey: Teacher' mental health declining amid job stress. Retrieved November 08, 2017, from www.usatoday.com/story/news/2017/10/30/survey-teachers-mental-health-declining-amid-jobstress/811577001/

Civics: The Study of the Rights and Duties of Citizenship

Katy Smith @KatyMN12, 2011 Minnesota Teacher of the Year, Parent Educator, Speaker, Author, and Advocate

I hear over and over from educators about how intimidated they are in their role as education advocates; so intimidated, in fact, that many of them never step into the work. Advocacy work, to so many, seems like something that other educational professionals, those with much more experience, more time, better resumes, more guts, or at the very least a minor in poly sci are engaged in. The truth is this, most of us come to advocacy work with little or no formal training.

Thankfully, very early in my career, I realized that advocacy work, at its very core, is about telling stories. I am full of stories, teachers are full of stories, administrators are full of stories, schools are full of stories, stories shape the culture and can shape policy (I have seen this with my own eyes!). Stories are powerful. Once, over lunch, I told the Governor a true story about a teacher colleague of mine. Mr. Reuter, an active duty serviceman, was responsible for paying his sub upon returning to the states because of a policy that was unfair to teachers. Later that year, I was in the room when the Governor signed the bill righting the injustice with Mr. Reuter at his side.

I was starstruck to meet Justice Sandra Day O'Connor in 2012. She was giving a keynote and I was in the audience. Justice O'Connor was at the podium in a ballroom full of teachers speaking about bringing civics education back into our social studies classrooms all across the state. Understanding our civic responsibility, she argued, is the foundation to a democratic society. She had me at "hello."

I come from a long line of folks who take their civic responsibility seriously. Those folks who talk politics at the dinner table, are the first to put yard signs in their lawn, never miss a voting day, and are happy to tell you who you should vote for, in case you haven't made up your mind. I follow the legislative process in the same way my son-in-law follows football.

When it comes right down to it, most of what we do in schools (everything we do in schools?) is a result of decisions made in our capital cities all across our nation by legislators. How long the school day is, the number of days in a school year, the per-pupil formula, and countless other operational decisions come from the collective effort of legislators, lobbyists, and the public to make schools work for students and their families. A few of those legislators are sworn in straight out of their classrooms, education leaders, inspired to move into policy work based on their experience in schools. Other legislators have not stepped into a school since they graduated from one (for a few, graduation day was a long, long, long time ago). And yet, their experience, their stories make up their understanding of how schools work, and are what drives education policy.

When it comes to advocacy work, the first assignment is knowing who represents you. Who are your school board members? Who is your state representative? Your state senator? Who is your Governor? Your Lieutenant Governor? Who represents you in Washington, D.C.? Who is your congressperson? Your senator? Your President? I'm serious, know who represents you. Google it if you need to, add them to your email contact list, sign up for their newsletter, add them to your Twitter feed, and send out a greeting. There, now you have a roster of folks who need to hear your stories. Share them. Share them on social media, over the phone, in person, over coffee in your hometown when they are there. Party affiliation makes no difference at this point. Once folks are elected, they represent you, even if their opinion does not.

The second assignment is to explore the landscape of policy influencers. Knowing what organizations are out there doing some of the same work that you care about can add some weight to your story and put policy on a fast track. I have been deeply concerned about the decline of play in childhood and in schools for many years now. When the American Association of Pediatrics released research on the importance of play in childhood in September of 2018, I was overjoyed. My stories about classrooms without play and the effect on children instantly became more powerful when paired with the new research. Stories, supported by research, forge promising avenues for creating public policy that benefit children. I want to be a part of that work.

Line up your advocacy work with what you are passionate about. Find folks who are doing similar work. Craft your story with a combination of real-life experience and research. Share that story and offer to be a part of the solution. Good public policy, all over the nation, has roots in someone's story, most of them involve a child. These stories are just waiting for a grown up to tell it and give it wings to make schools better for children.

Want to know more?

Who to Follow:
Your advocacy work is work that is close to your heart and very personal. Your list of who to follow will reflect your passion. Here is a suggestion of how to get started.
Your governor
Your legislators
Advocates you admire
Organizations who do the work

Additional Resources:
http://pediatrics.aappublications.org/content/142/3/e20182058
The hashtag that connects you to the cause and its advocates.

Takeaways for Tomorrow

See a need, fill a need. Instead of asking community partners to come into the school – try going out. Volunteer at a local event, support local businesses, attend city council meetings, and meet with local legislators. Spending time and investing within the community offers opportunities to find intentional partnerships that value all perspectives and offer authentic opportunities to enhance our partnerships.

Write a letter, attend a meeting, be an advocate. By connection with NAESP/NASSP and their advocacy platform and resources you can become knowledgeable about local and national resources to enhance the voice you have.

What you post is your priority. What you tweet and what you state when you say it makes a difference. How often, what, and why you post to your social media sites shows stakeholders your priorities, your values, and offers them insight into what you do day to day and how they can help. Tagging local legislators or business partners that had a role in the event or picture continues to enhance the message and value the partners that are a part of it.

A Few Final Thoughts

Inspired yet? There are incredible partnerships literally right across the street from your school. Leadership from a lens of community and legislative partnerships provides a new opportunity to reach a population that traditionally has felt like an afterthought – now you can ensure the work they do with you is a value add for the school and your students. With all this knowledge of unconventional ways to make more meaningful connections we have saved the most important chapter for last. Creating ways to unplug from the world of work and plug into your own wellbeing.

Social Media Mantra

- Living and leading within the community you serve reaches far beyond the title on your business card – it becomes who you are. **#UnConLeader**
- What you post is how you show others what is important. **#UnConLeader**

Create your own! Use the hashtag #UnConLeader to share your own takeaways.

CHALLENGE

AFTER READING THIS CHAPTER I AM INTRIGUED BY THIS TOPIC:

I WILL LEARN MORE BY FOLLOWING THESE #UnConLeaders:

TAKE A PICTURE OF YOUR LEARNING WORK IN ACTION!
USE THE HASHTAG SO WE CAN LEAD TOGETHER!

#UnConLeader

Want to Learn More?

Loria, R. (2018, March 25). A how-to guide for building school-community partnerships. *EdWeek*. Retrieved from www.edweek.org/ew/articles/2018/03/23/a-how-to-guide-for-building-school-community-partnerships.html. Accessed February 20, 2019.

NAESP and NASSP. (2013). Leadership matters (2013). Retrieved from www.naesp.org/sites/default/files/LeadershipMatters.pdf. Accessed February 20, 2019.

Stoll, M. (2017, February 23). Mentor and a story – 'Everybody Wins' turns another page in Austin. *Austin Daily Herald*. Retrieved from www.austindailyherald.com/2017/02/mentor-and-a-story-everybody-wins-turns-another-page-in-austin/. Accessed February 19, 2019.

Leading for Yourself

This chapter is intentionally the last one. School leadership is complicated, emotionally exhausting, and utterly rewarding at the same time. Becoming great at what you do in your day job requires you to take a break from it at night and at other times.

But who has the time for self-care? In a study by Bono and colleagues (2013) participants recorded three good things that happened that day and why they thought that good thing happened. Just that small intentional act produced positive results.

Valerie Brown and Kirsten Olson (2015) found that within the context of a chaotic and challenging educational leadership environment, most leaders do not prioritize time for renew and recharge for themselves. Too often we place value on the outputs and products we produce for others, not the inputs we need for our wellbeing. Surviving over thriving is something I have heard over and over and experienced myself.

In *Balance Like A Pirate* (2018) we tried to convey that self-care is not selfish. In this work, self-care is not only not selfish, it can be lifesaving. Just google "School Leaders and Self Care," we are working on it and working towards it ... and we know it is essential in order to thrive in the strive and struggle of the work.

The work of self-care is essential for every school staff member. Jeffrey Benson (2017) shares that teacher self-care is a solution to the demands of teaching every child, regardless of their mental health needs. Secondary trauma is now discussed in schools with as much importance as academic rigor, standards, and instruction. The issues are right in front of us, and we need to create a space to address them before we lose anymore educators because of it.

Educators are moving into a new era of learning and leading the future leaders. And if we do not equip each other with self-care strategies that are implemented on a regular basis, the outlook is not promising. Retention of those with the biggest hearts and brightest futures could be burned out sooner than any of us want to see.

This chapter will give specific strategies and research behind separating your work life and home life and how doing this regularly will make you better at both. Moving forward, remember: in order to help others, you absolutely need to take care of yourself, first.

We may be superheros,

BUT WE ARE NOT MADE OF STEEL.

#UNCONLEADER

Linking the Learning

Setting Limits so You Can Soar

This is tough work. I will be honest; more than once this school year I have questioned my worth in the work and if I am enough or even if I can keep up at this pace. Leadership can also feel isolating, and not checked can lead to senses of fear, mistrust, and breakdown relationships quicker than any school initiative implemented poorly. Don Miguel Ruiz (1997) shares four agreements that can translate easily to healthy boundaries for school leaders.

- **Be impeccable with your word**. Words matter and the tone and timing of when you say what you say is equally important. This also translated into electronic communication. At times I have to put myself in check before responding to an email when I myself might not be regulated enough to respond in a kind and caring manner. Most times it has little to do with the content in the email, more so it has to do with my own attitude prior to opening the inbox. If you are answering emails on your phone (well, stop – but that is another topic), if it is anything that comes with conflict or a sense of frustration from the other party – wait and respond on a computer. Taking the time to respond to a courageous conversation when you are fully focused and not multitasking in the lunchroom could make all the difference between building relationships or building up a higher wall.
- **Don't take anything personally**. No seriously. Each educator walks into the building with their own stories, own challenges, and values of what is important. I learned this over and over my first year leading a school campus. For months I kept thinking, why is everyone "questioning" every decision I make? Do they not think I can do the job? Do they think they can do it better? Are they talking about me when I am out of the room? Yes, it spiraled quickly out of control in my head.

  Do you want to know why they really asked the questions? Because they wanted me to succeed and were worried I might not know all the history and the depth to decision making. They quizzed me because they wanted me to be successful – not to drive me out (or crazy).

- **Don't make assumptions.** 2 + 2 doesn't always equal 4 if you don't consider the variables in the equation. If I am stressed my immediate reaction is to become argumentative and defensive. Leading up to our first big incentive at a school I was leading my stress got the better of me and instead of asking if I was misreading cues and comments I went to the dark side and assumed everyone wanted this to fail, or worse yet they thought I was the failure. With that mental mantra in my thought bubble, you can only imagine the words that came out of my talk bubble. Not great. If you have a question about intention of another it is simple: ask them. Nine times out of ten you are completely out of base and the other person will clarify quickly and the situation de-escalates, and you can leave feeling heard, and so much better.

- **Always do your best.** Our school mantra during the 2018–19 school year was "Expect the Best" and how can you argue that one? Looking at the situation with positive intention will always lead towards a better outcome than walking in with a negative or "gotcha" attitude. As a leader I wanted to lead as a "I got you" if you fall instead of a "gotcha" leader when you fail. Want to build a base of best intentions? It is easy – compliment others' attempts. By celebrating the steps towards success, the missteps are more easily set aside so you can focus on doing better, every day.

Caught Up, Stuck In, Bogged Down

Leaders are on all the time. In the halls, by the office, in the summer, at the movie with friends, walking down the grocery aisles. I have even run into families on a vacation, hundreds of miles away from home. While hanging a sign around our neck out of school saying "do not disturb" is not socially acceptable, there are unconventional ways you can set boundaries and build relationships at the same time.

Getting caught up, stuck in, or bogged down in the task, conversations and circumstances out of your control can translate into a response that it is out of character, out of control, and not productive. Trust me, I have seen and done more of these unproductive behaviors when I am taking on too much. This rang so true that my first secretary commissioned a piece of art that still hides behind my computer that says "sometimes I throw pens" well, because when I am stressed ... I do. In *Balance Like a Pirate* (Cabeen et al. 2018) we call this emotional response the Five Steps of Freaking Out, and not put in check can totally put you right over the edge.

- The first step is a calm reaction and response to a situation. This is when the wheels are the bus in our personal and professional life.
- The next step is controlling. If I only worked a little later, finished that report, rewrote an article, then life would resume back in order. Notice the calibration is starting to shift and at least one wheel on the bus is going flat.
- The third step up is self-deprecation, a place I live in too often and too well. We diminish our own worth in the work as a way to deflect the issues or refuse to look at the root cause. Now we are working with two flat tires and the frame is starting to crack.
- Next up irrational response. No one listens, let's just give every student a flip phone and shut off Wi-Fi in the entire building. These responses are fueled by lack of sleep, lack of support, and lack of a willingness to reach out and ask for help from trusted friends in the work.
- The final step is the outburst, the internal or external three-year-old temper tantrum. For some of us it is a full-on blow out on someone just walking by; for others the tears start to stream over the smallest thing. Whatever the response the next step on the process is a full-fledged fall.

Recognizing our hot buttons or finding someone who can call you out when you are sending emails way too late or too early will help regain the balance you need to do the work well. Achor (2010) states that taking on too much and not taking a break from it can cause a and emotional and physical response that signals the sky is falling, when really it isn't.

#UnConLeader Twitter Connections

People to Follow:

Sarah Johnson @SarahSajohnson

Website: https://sarahsajohnson.com/

Jessica Johnson @PrincipalJ

Website: www.principalj.net/

Amber Teamann @8Amber8

www.amberteamann.com/

Principal Productivity (Facebook Group): www.facebook. com/groups/principalproductivity/

Angela Watson @Angela_Watson

Podcast: https://thecornerstoneforteachers.com/ truth-for-teachers-podcast/

Hashtags to Watch:

#TruthforTeachers

#BalanceLAP

#UnConLeader Keys

How can you find intentional time and ways to step away from the work and step into a space to regroup, renew, and recharge?

Who can hold you accountable? How can you share your strategies and influence others to make time and space for self-care?

Do it Right, or Do it Now

School leaders have to make swift decisions, and many times we do so without 100% of the information. Discipline, field trips, incentives, impromptu parent meetings, and the list goes on and on. And while sometimes our responses have to be immediate, it is important to not that let that become your routine. Daniel Kahneman (2011) explains modes of thinking into two systems: System 1 operates automatically and quickly, with little or no effort and no sense of voluntary control; System 2 allocates attention to the effortful mental activities that demand it, including complex computations. Some decisions need to be made with all the information, more stakeholder input, and a little collaboration with colleagues or your PLN.

I experienced this within weeks of starting a new position leading a middle school. And while I had been in this building seven years prior as the assistant principal, many things had changed as well as my viewpoint from my position of leadership. Staff were asking for clear cut rules of grading.

How many assessments, percentage for practice work vs assessments, clear parameters on what counts as an assessment, and what I planned to do with students who just didn't do anything?

I could have just given yes/no's right away in August – that would have gotten these questions off my plate, pleased the people I just started working with, and that would have been it. But I didn't do that. In October the conversation came back, how do we "know" what constitutes a student who has alternate grading vs one who doesn't? Why don't you just put back academic consequences for missing work? Why are we not talking about grade level retention and identifying students like we have done before?

The longer I waited to make decisions on these questions the clearer the actual issue became. Yes, we needed to re-calibrate our why and practices in grading at the middle school, but we also needed to talk about student motivation, the role homework has in our school, and how to relook at our teaching strategies to incorporate more student-centered involvement and less lecture-style sit and learn from the teacher in school. Had I just started making decisions in August the snowball would have just gotten bigger and I would never have remembered what rule I set, who I said it to, and how in the world I was going to support the accountability of each practice. Instead we waited, I listened, and in the spring we will be forming a grading committee to look at the different aspects of a "grade": how it impacts student instruction, learning, and what types of professional development will be helpful in establishing these practices as standard work in our school.

The Stress of Teaching our Students

This work is worth it, but it is hard. Teaching today's students means we work with what walks into our schools, and that can change by the minute, hour, or day. Researchers have defined this new stressor to service as secondary traumatic stress.

In an article by Jessica Lander (2018), she stresses that schools that have staff impacted by secondary traumatic stress should provide them with resources and make clear that symptoms are not a sign of weakness, but an indicator that they might need support because they work in an challenging profession.

Leaders today need to prioritize identifying these symptoms in their staff and find ways to incorporate opportunities for self-care and fewer ways to isolate themselves when experiencing this trauma. Where is the best place to start? Look in the mirror. Teachers will be more apt to start to engage in self-care practices if their leader is modeling the work. I used to state with staff that there is not a prize for the person who stays the latest or longest each day. But until I modeled that practice myself, the cars stayed late and the stress piled up. Now I ask staff to hold me accountable to my family, which includes reminding me when it is time to leave as well.

Be honest. Teachers are not looking for a perfect leader – seriously. The more honest, transparent, and real we can be, peels the layers off quicker so we can get into a trusted relationship and do the right work in the right way. Maybe an interaction with a student went wrong, or you left a meeting with a teacher and you felt a little more tension leaving than arriving. Circle back and reflect together, ask for feedback, and lean into what others have to say. The more honest and open conversations about how hard this work is will allow us to learn and grow together to be better for our students, and ourselves.

#UnConLeader Twitter Connections

People to Follow:
Clay Cook @ClayCook_phd
Website: http://itr.umn.edu/clay-cook/
LaVonna Roth @LaVonnaRoth
Website: www.igniteyourshine.com/
Allyson Apsey @AllysonApsey
Website: https://allysonapsey.com/
Kelley Begley McCall @Mccall_kelley
Website: http://aninspiredprincipal.blogspot.com/
James Moffett @JamesMoffettJr

Hashtags to Watch:
#traumainformed
#InAwetoRise
#principalinbalance
#PowerofPositiveSummit

#UnConLeader Keys
What work has been done, or could be used, to inform staff about the importance of self-care in the work of caring for our kids?
How can you embed these strategies into the day and professional development for staff?

Know When to Grow, or Go

Forks in your career road can either elevate your life and career or send you into a spiral of frustration, self-doubt, and burnout. Multiple times in my adult life I have been approached by my mentors and supervisors for new opportunities and challenges. Early on I always said yes. Yes to a new school, a new teaching assignment, a cohort masters program, and an administrative position.

As I grew in my own professional and personal beliefs, I started to weigh more on what I wanted, not necessarily what others wanted me to be. In the past ten years I have said NO to two offers – both no's would seem to fly in the face of reason. The titles alone in these new positions were more prestigious, offered more financial security, and would have elevated professional status. But yet I said no, thank you. Timing plays a part, but by leading unconventionally, taking the road less traveled is more likely the route you will choose.

Letting go of something good in search of something great is a scary decision. But sometimes comfort can be a curse – a way to stay in sameness and not grow, take risks, or innovate your leadership style. In a study done by the US Department of Education (2018) of public school principals who agreed strongly or somewhat with the statement "I think about transferring to another school" in the 2015–16 school year, 12 percent left the principal-ship and 12 percent moved to a different school in 2016–17. You are not alone in looking for something different, and sometimes that move is the best thing you can do for your own self-care.

Decisions around leaving are sometimes due to circumstances of a toxic culture out of your control (more in the next section). If a supervisor or significant circumstance is challenging and changing the core of who you are – it is time to go.

More challenging choices might be staying in a position because you were promised, or hoping to get, something else in the district down the road. If you are waiting in the wings, but not growing in the positions you are currently in and complaining to others about who is in the seat you want – start applying elsewhere. Those negative thoughts unchecked turn into negative talk and can actually damage a culture you created in your current context and could damage the changes of that other choice down the road.

Unconventional leaders ask and listen to others for advice in the big decisions. For my first voice is my spouse, and if it passes him it might be our kids, a trusted retired friend, or my tribe of leaders that I call from across the country. I talk to them about the opportunity and ask for the honest truth. And then I go to my core leadership beliefs to see if this could be a fit. These include:

1. Who am I and how do I want to be known as a leader?
2. Will this opportunity elevate my calling?
3. Does this position provide opportunity to challenge and help me grow?
4. Does the culture and beliefs of the school align with my own style?

Leading in today's schools is more complex, challenging, and high stakes than ever before. Ensuring you are ready, willing, and excited for the invitation is critical for your own self-care and for the care of the school community.

When to Leave It in Your Car, When to Leave It in Your School: Setting the Boundaries around Self-Care at School and Home

I can remember it clearly, I was tired, the holidays were coming. The planning and preparation for holiday programs, data meetings in the new year, and registration for the next class had me burning the candle at all ends. Earlier in the week I had to have a tough conversation with a parent about their child's tardies to school and the impact that had on the learning. That morning the police showed up at the school to tell me that same parent had just been hospitalized due to an attempt on their own life and the outcome was not looking great. I took a deep breathe, grabbed my coat, and went to my car, I called my good friend who was a principal at another school in the district and cried. What had I done? What can I do know? How can I walk back into school with a smile on my face knowing one of our students is going home to a completely different circumstance that when he arrived? That friend literally let me lose it on the phone, walked me back to sanity, and helped me regroup so I could go back and do my best that day to keep the systems moving smoothly for everyone. Maya Angelou (2008) states this approach so well: "You may not control all the events that happen to you, but you can decide not to be reduced by them."

In that instance I learned the importance of setting boundaries on what consumes my thoughts and what drives my day. Finding that friend to help me process through the situation helped me to know what my next steps would be going back into school being so close to the situation. And the hardest part of that day – leaving what happened when I parked my car in the garage that night and going into the house to assume the titles of wife and mother. Leaving it in your car is a way to provide self-care and protect those you care about from the heartbreak of the job that we love. If you can't separate from it, it can consume you and leave you empty, sad, and unaware how to recalibrate.

If You Are Not Happy ... Leave

Here is the tough one: you may be in a situation in which your own mental health is in jeopardy due to a toxic climate, leadership, or community. It could be a new leader joining the ranks with very different views than your own. It could be taking a new position for the "title" but walking into a school that doesn't agree with how you lead. Maybe you stuck it out for a few years and now your day includes the toxic behaviors that seen anywhere else you would leave, but now it seems normal. If a situation is changing you for the worse, impacting your health, and help isn't available, sometimes the best course is to leave.

Now just because you left one position doesn't mean you won't be better in another. Unconventional leadership means sometimes the road less traveled is the one you have to take. Never sacrifice your core beliefs for a nameplate on a door. Find a trusted friend, spouse, or somewhen who knew the you before this and ask the question – have I changed? And if so, for the better or the worse? If you can hear the answer, then act on it if necessary. I have watched too many new leaders stick it out in a position that wasn't meant to be for them, but because they were too afraid of what others might think, they stick around, and in turn lose more of who they dreamed to be.

#UnConLeader Twitter Connections

People to Follow:
Michael Hyatt @MichaelHyatt
Website: https://michaelhyatt.com/
Simon Sinek @Simonsinek
Website: https://startwithwhy.com/
Andy Jacks @_AndyJacks
Website: https://andyjacks.co/
Danny Bauer @alienearbud_
Website: www.betterleadersbetterschools.com/

Hashtags to Watch:
#CelebrateMonday
#JoyfulLeaders
#PowerOfPositiveSummit
#fitleaders
#BLBS

Other Places to Check Out:
www.betterleadersbetterschools.com/podcast/
Mel Robbins: https://melrobbins.com/
Rachel Hollis on Instagram @msrachelhollis
Website: https://thechicsite.com/
Gretchen Rubin Happier Podcast: https://gretchenrubin.com/podcasts/

#UnConLeader Keys

Take time to reflect and write down who you are and how you want to lead:
Who am I and how do I want to be known as a leader?
Regularly assess if what you are doing now will get you to where you want to be and be known as a leader.

Leaders in the Field

Married to the Job

Leslie Kapuchuck, Elementary Principal in Rockingham County, Va. @LKapuchuck

J. Kapuchuck, Elementary Principal in Rockingham County, Va. @PrincipalKap

The typical principal's spouse has to make many sacrifices in order to be supportive of the principal's role in the school community. When you are a principal, and you're married to another principal, balancing work life and family life can be a major challenge. We are in a constant state of juggling work, home, and family, while having two children in elementary school. Did we mention they attend a separate elementary school from those in which we lead and serve each day?

Between the two of us, we work with nearly 1,000 students, 200 staff members, and countless parents and community members. At the same time, we have to make sure our two children are a priority. For as long as they can remember, we have been in leadership roles. This has required us to spend a lot of time away from our home and family, resulting in at least one of us missing milestones, important family events, watching our children receive awards at school, as well as their sporting events. Our evenings and weekends often consist of meetings and late-night events, so we show up with our children in tow. This allows us to be present for our schools, and also for our own children. Our hope is that bringing them along with us will teach them that we all have responsibilities and that we have to show up for the people we serve, no matter what. We would be lying if we said there wasn't a bit of guilt associated with this!

Meeting our commitments to our jobs, our kids, and each other isn't easy, but we've found ways that work for us. On a typical weeknight, we are texting each other to see who will be picking up the kids and who will be taking care of dinner. We usually meet at home around 6 pm and have dinner as a family. During this time, we are spending quality time together, away from cell phones and our computers. We find ourselves discussing our children's school days, and often end up discussing our own. However, as our children are getting older, they are involved in their own extracurricular activities. While one of us may be picking up our son to take him to a sports practice, the other is doing the same for our daughter. On nights when we are going in different directions, we finally come together as a family around 8 pm and it's time for nightly routines and bed for our children. Then it's back to school work for us.

When you're a true servant leader, and you're passionate about your job, you want to give 100% to everyone you serve, all of the time. We both value our role as lead learners, therefore most of our time is spent out of our office and interacting with our students and staff. We try to complete the managerial tasks of our jobs in the evenings after our children go to bed. We are constantly collaborating with and pushing each other out of our comfort zones in order to move our schools forward.

We have learned that we are better leaders and parents when we are able to step away from work mode at a decent hour. We have both learned from experience that we can't continue to push ourselves to work until exhaustion. Spot checking email during the school day, prioritizing the "to do" list when we arrive at work each morning, having a mobile desk at work, delegating tasks, and learning to say "no" has allowed us to balance work and home life. We have both embraced the fact that being a workaholic isn't good for our family.

Despite being intentional in our daily routines, we do still find it difficult to balance work and having a personal life. One thing we have found helpful is to take vacation time when our children are out of school. We try to take a vacation over spring break and at least one family vacation in the summer. Getting away from home allows us to enjoy family time without interruptions. These vacations also allow us to recharge, reflect, and make memories as a family. Even though we are on vacation, we might be sitting in our beach chairs discussing how we are going to make our schools even better for our students and our staff. It's difficult to truly unplug from work when there are two principals in the family who are so passionate about their roles!

We have been working through this for the past five years and we are still trying to figure out the best way to balance work and family life. Being a principal requires a lot of passion, dedication, and a true desire to continue learning and growing each day. We both view our roles as an opportunity rather than an obligation and while it's never easy to find balance, we want our son and daughter to be confident that they are our number one priority and that will never change.

Want to Know More?

Who to Follow:
Andy Jacks @_AndyJacks
Hamish Brewer @brewerhm
Mark French @PrincipalFrench
Todd Nesloney @TechNinjaTodd
Beth Houf @BethHouf
Brad Gustafson @GustafasonBrad

Additional Resources:
Better Leaders Better Schools

Rise, Shine, and Lead

Nick Proud, @Nick_Proud, Principal Garner Elementary, FinestGreatestBest.com, and cofounder of #DadsAsPrincipals

Each morning begins at 4:48 am. Why 4:48? Why such a weird time? It is because of balance. If I get up at exactly 4:48 am, my wife is already done getting ready and on her way to a 5:00 am workout class. This allows me to check my email to make sure we have enough substitutes for the day. If we have enough subs, I have a few extra minutes. If not, the scramble begins. My goal is to begin my workout no later than 5:20 am. I quickly scroll social media and read my daily devotional in the YouVersion Bible app. My workout must be completed by 6:20, so I have time to empty the dishwasher and grab my opening cup of coffee before heading upstairs to get ready for the day. By 7:00 am both kids, my wife, and I need to be in the kitchen packing lunches and discussing the day. Every morning, I make breakfast for the family and not just bowls of cereal but a real, hot breakfast. I am famous for my chocolate chip pancakes, but those are reserved for the weekend. This fine-tuned symphony results in the kids loaded in the car with me as we head to school no later than 7:20 am.

You may be wondering why I would go into so much detail about our morning, but it is because of balance. There are two moments that are very special to me in this schedule. First, the calm before the storm. As I sit and read before I work out, it is one of the most peaceful times of my day. The house is quiet, and it is me and my thoughts. As a principal, those moments do not happen often, so I cherish the peace before my day begins.

Second is making breakfast. A former colleague of mine shared with me that one of her favorite memories was her dad making breakfast every morning no matter how busy he was. At the time, I didn't think much of it because my daughter was little, and my son wasn't yet born. But now I understand. As I scramble the eggs, toast a waffle, or pour some milk I am able to connect with my kids. On some days that might be the best, or only conversation, we have all day as our schedules push us in opposite directions. I enjoy providing my wife with a delicious start to her day as a way of saying thank you and I love you. It may seem simple and not that much time, but for me and my family, it is balance. It is joy. It is how our family works. Having this as an anchor to our lives creates a structure that allows our days to go.

Throughout the rest of the day, my balance comes from little checkpoints that positively interrupt the hectic nature of a principal's day. One of my favorite checkpoints is stopping by to see my kids during their lunch. Often this includes me dropping a piece of candy into their lunchboxes. Many times, very few words are shared, but it is a moment that we all enjoy. It is a small sign of love that can turn around the most difficult day.

These checkpoints were increasingly important in the past two years of my life while I was taking classes for my superintendent's advanced study certificate, completing over 900 internship hours while leading the largest elementary school in my district of nearly 700 students. During this busy time, these small checkpoints became ever more important as each minute of the day seemed to be accounted for. Whether it is a dinner with the family, a serious Mario Cart 8 battle, or reading to my kids before bed, these checkpoints provide balance and an opportunity to focus on what is important.

Want to Know More?

Who to Follow:
George Curous @gcouros
Amber Teamann @8amber8
Todd Whitaker @ToddWhitaker
Joe Sanfelippo @Joe_Sanfelippo
Jessica Cabeen @JessicaCabeen

Where to Find Out More:
Check out my blog at http://proudspoints.blogspot.com/
My professional website www.finestgreatestbest.com
Check out @DadsAsPrincipal on Twitter

Juggling Priorities

Lindsy Stumpenhorst @Principalboots Principal, @Momsasprincipal co-founder
  https://principalinboots.wordpress.com/
  https://itunes.apple.com/us/podcast/power-struggle-podcast/id1341688161?mt=2

"Mrs. Stumpenhorst, your son is sick, I need you to come pick him up."

I had three students in my office, a parent on hold, and was 45 minutes away from my son's school. This was my first year as an assistant principal at a middle school and I was doing a pretty good job at managing my professional life. The problem was it felt as though my personal life was spiraling out of control.

Working. Mom. Keeping these two full-time jobs straight is hard, add into the mix my newly accepted administrative position, and it was nearly impossible. There may have even been a day that I sent my son to school in pajamas after getting our two school calendars mixed up. The good thing? He was only in 2nd grade and didn't mind going to school in his PJ's, in fact, he was quite impressed with the fact that he was the ONLY person who wore pajamas to school that day.

During my second administrative year, I was offered the opportunity to transfer to a 3rd–5th grade school as the principal. After encouragement from my #momsasprincipals tribe, I knew how I was going to balance these two worlds. The Stumpenhorst family was going all in. All in for us means embedding ourselves in the community. Our son was going to be in third grade and our daughter was going to be in kindergarten. If there was a big decision to be made … it was now. With a strong will and a positive attitude my husband and I broke the news to the kids that for the new school year, they would be attending a different school district.

From the in-town salon or barbershop that we cut our hair, to the spirit wear hanging in the closet, we truly did go all in. I attend parent-teacher conferences as a principal and a mom, the same for field trips and after school activities. This unique circumstance of open enrolling to Sterling Public Schools has given me an opportunity to be successful at both being a mom and being a principal. I don't have to choose between either, because usually I'm balancing both.

I'm blessed to be surrounded by the most compassionate and family orientated school district; they have truly embraced the entire Stumpenhorst family. An added benefit of mixing my professional and personal life is that to those around me I'm real, not untouchable, imperfect, and additionally approachable. I make mistakes, usually with an audience, although with help from my favorite blogging principals Rachael Peck and Liz Garden I continue to grow and learn.

To lead a household and a school I have many tips and tricks, but the most powerful tool I use is reflection. I reflect through writing on my own blog, PrincipalinBoots, and recording with my husband on our Power Struggle Podcast. The transparency of blogging and podcasting will hopefully inspire others to not seek perfection but growth. I've seen this growth through reading posts by Moms As Principals' member Cindy Emmerson, on her Lead Vibes website. Emmersizzle (as we call her) rocks it on a daily basis for her school family.

Commuting to school and open enrolling my kids isn't always sunshine and rainbows; some days are long, sometimes the long drive seems to take days, and on the rare occasion we even mention aloud the benefits of attending the local school. Aside from brief moments, the adjustment my family has made in an attempt to help me juggle being a mom and a principal is working. Four years later, my son is now in middle school. He is appreciative of his time in a different building and has quickly realized that this freedom also comes with zero "mom saves the day" moments. My daughter is in third grade, at my school, and there have been some growing pains associated with the understanding that even though I'm your mom AND principal, while at school I don't just have one kid, but 400.

Want to Know More?

Who to Follow:
Rachael Peck @rachaelpeck23
Liz Garden @principalgarden
Cindy Emmerson @Emersizzle

Additional Resources:
Rachaelpeck.blogspot.com
Growingwithprincipalgarden.wordpress.com
http://leadvibes.blogspot.com/

Life with Two Married School Administrators

Heidi Veal, Early Childhood Program Administrator, @VealHeidi
  Jeff Veal, Middle School Assistant Principal, @heffrey
  Jeff and I are both public school administrators, wild right?! In different districts and in dramatically different roles, but administrators all the same. As you can imagine, this has led to many interesting conversations over the past five years, but in all honesty these conversations have been a part of our life together for as long as I can remember. For the 25 years Jeff and I have known each other, our passion for serving others vocationally has been something that always brought us together. It was one of the core things that drew us to one another in the first place as students at Harding University, where we met, dated, and were engaged. While students at Harding, our passion for teaching grew – Jeff in the church setting ministering to students and families and me via elementary education with an emphasis in early childhood and student ministries. During our college years, we both served middle and high school students via church ministries throughout a mixture of internships, summers away at camp, and university-sponsored mission trips and events.

  We married two weeks after graduating from Harding and were overjoyed to step into our first jobs, side-by-side, which was something we never expected or pursued, but were beyond thrilled when it happened by surprise! To back up a little, Heidi was poised, prepped, and ready to enter her first teaching job. She had her heart set on teaching kindergarten or first grade and even had a job offer at a great private school in Houston, but as things worked out, God had other plans for us in Dallas. Jeff interviewed with a church in the heart of Dallas and before we knew it, they were offering not just Jeff a job, but Heidi too! They wanted to bring us both on as co-student ministers. We served in this capacity for the first two years we were married, sharing every component of the ministry's work from mission trips and summer camps, to Bible study, curriculum design and teaching, all the way down to an office, computer, desk phone ... you get the picture.

  Little did we know these first two years would foreshadow so much of our lives together. After the two years we worked together with the church in Dallas, we moved to Pflugerville, north of Austin, to work with a church plant where Jeff was on staff as their associate pastor and Heidi began her official public-school teaching career. Since then, she remained in public schools, as a teacher, instructional coach, assistant principal, and today serving as the early childhood administrator for a large North Texas school district. Jeff, after many years of leading thriving church-based student ministries, transitioned into public education to teach fourth grade and later middle school robotics and social studies. Jeff currently serves as a middle school assistant principal in the fastest growing school district in Texas.

Now you know our story of what brought us to where we are today. Many people laugh and look at us like we are a little on the crazy side when we tell them we are both school administrators with two young boys at home. I'll share with you a few of our secrets for making marriage and family life work when both mom and dad serve in leadership roles in two different school districts.

Faith

First, we have always had faith that our love for serving and teaching would guide our lives together. And that it has. We have always been dedicated first to our home team and hold onto faith that if we lead our family well, the rest will fall into place. There is a time and place to let work stay at work so that we can play for the home team. It means saying that difficult word "no" to overextending ourselves to other commitments that may impede this first priority. Always keep the right thing, the main thing. We know we are modeling for the people in our care that value and trust us – they do appreciate it!

And Trust

Speaking of trust – though we could have never predicted exactly where our callings would lead us, we knew it would align to a higher purpose and that we would be taken care of because we are fulfilling what we have been made to do. We trust our calling and we trust each other, no matter what. We know that we don't make decisions as an individual, but as a Team Veal and as an entire family, seeking to put the needs of the family above all. This means even on the hardest of days assuming positive intent on the part of the other person.

Not Pixie Dust, but Hard Work

We have always worked hard for everything. We cheer each other on in our endeavors and pursue big dreams together. That's why it made perfect sense to us when we both went to grad school at the same time, though it was at two different schools and I was pregnant with our second son. At that time, we were both serving in public schools and it worked for us. We helped and supported one another; talking about our classes, exchanging experiences, studying for certification exams, and cheering one another on at our respective graduation ceremonies. We continue to work hard in our professional roles, but more importantly in our most important role as parents. We are not perfect parents, but we give it our best.

Shared Mission

We believe with our hearts that what we do is a calling, knowing the work we do is too important and the stakes are too high for the students we serve. At the core, it's ministry. We serve students, families, teachers, and schools vocationally with a heart to please God, not men. We hope we are modeling this well for our boys. Some days we do and other days we fail. This is missional work filled with challenges and celebrations. We strive to understand that the mission is both personal and professional, it is who we are!

Want to Know More?

Who to Follow:	Additional Resources:
@PrincipalPaul	Check out our blog jhveal.com and the #LeadUpTeach
@drneilgupta	podcast on iTunes and YouTube.
@ElisaBostwick	Follow @LeadUpNow, #LeadUpChat and #ECEchat on
@tsschmidty	Twitter, weekly education Twitter chats, co-founded
@AmyHeavin	respectively by Jeff and Heidi.
@Wes_Kieschnick	Podcasts that we have been featured on to learn more
@DrPowersKHS &	include Bam Radiostudentcentricty; KidsDesevelt; Better
@drpowers1	Leaders, Better Schools; Aspire Leadership; Principally
	Speaking; and Teaching Keating.

DEDICATING TIME TO YOUR MARRIAGE IS MORE IMPORTANT THAN DEDICATING TIME TO YOUR CAREER

YOUR CAREER IS TEMPORARY, YOUR RELATIONSHIPS ARE FOREVER.

#UNCONLEADER

Takeaways for Tomorrow

Focus. "If you give your mind something meaningful to do through-out all your waking hours, you'll end the day more fulfilled and begin the next one more relaxed," Newport (2016). With that in mind, set intentions each morning for the day ahead. I have utilized a format in which each morning after a devotional I look at my day ahead and list three things I will accomplish. It could be walkthroughs, observations, hallway supervision, or completing a budget report that has been sitting on my desk. I intentionally block out time to accomplish these tasks – without distraction.

What is your ideal week? Danny Bauer speaks, lives, and supports educators in developing their ideal week. Being a productive leader means you have to have a plan. He believes in this so much he offers the template as a free resource on his website: https://betterleaders-betterschools.com/time-blocking-template/.

Unplug. Okay, I kind of wish I had a blocking tool on my phone like I put on my son's to limit his time on Instagram and Snapchat. If you struggle with regulating your time with your phone, and like all of us, multi-tasking is a myth … shut it down. Seriously, put it in another room, shut it off, or give it to your spouse. Not looking at your phone, your email, or other distractions for long periods of the day will allow you to focus on the tasks at hand and have them completed in a more clear and complete fashion.

Sleep. Find your internal clock and go with it. Early bird? Go to bed at a reasonable time, so you can get up ready to go the next day. Set a regular routine for consistency, even on the weekends! As a mom of a tween and teen, my Saturday mornings are super productive as my 5 am alarm goes off and the boys are still asleep till 9 – 4 hours of reflection, reading, and a bike ride before they even get up!

Set a timer. My friend Adam Welcome helped me with this one when I was working on my application for the Digital Leader of Early Learning. I kept looking at it, reading, rereading, and procrastinating on sending. He finally said to set a timer for 30 minutes, make final adjustments, and hit send. Be careful with all the tasks and to-do's on your plate that you don't procrastinate without a purpose and end time in mind.

Stop, drop and go! Have you caught yourself delaying or being late to a personal commitment over a work task? When your kids call for a pick up, your spouse asks you out, or you notice that you are almost late to dinner, but have that one … last … email. Stop working, drop what you are doing, and go home.

A Few Final Thoughts

Educators are superheroes, not superhuman. Recognizing the need to recharge and support each other in the work of self-care will only strengthen the work of the organization. Take intentional time as a school and district to find unconventional ways to focus on the health of those who serve our students. The investment will be worth the effort.

Social Media Mantra

- We may be superheroes, but we are not made of steel. **#UnConLeader**
- Dedicating time to your marriage is more important than dedicating time to your career; your career is temporary, your relationships are forever. **#UnConLeader**

Create your own! Use the hashtag #UnConLeader to share your own takeaways.

CHALLENGE

AFTER READING THIS CHAPTER I AM INTRIGUED BY THIS TOPIC:

I WILL LEARN MORE BY FOLLOWING THESE #UnConLeaders:

TAKE A PICTURE OF YOUR LEARNING WORK IN ACTION!
USE THE HASHTAG SO WE CAN LEAD TOGETHER!

Want to Learn More?

Achor, S. (2010). *The happiness advantage.* New York: Crown Publishing.

Angelou, M. (2008). *Letter to my daughter.* New York: Random House.

Benson, J. (2017). When teacher self-care is not enough. *Educational Leadership, 75*(4), 38–42.

Bondo, J., Glomb, T., Shen, W., Kim, E., & Kock, A. (2013). Building positive resources: Effects of positive events and positive reflections on work stress and health. *Academy of Management Journal, 56*(6), 1601–1627.

Brown, V., & Olson, K. (2018). *The mindful school leader: Practices to transform your leadership and your school.* Thousand Oaks, CA: Corwin.

Cabeen, J., Johnson, J., & Johnson, S. (2018). *Balance like a pirate.* San Diego, CA: Dave Burgess Consulting, Inc.

Kahneman, D. (2011). *Thinking fast, thinking slow.* New York: Farrar, Straus and Giroux.

Lander, J. (2018, September 26). Helping teachers manage the weight of trauma. [Blog post] Retrieved from www.gse.harvard.edu/news/uk/18/09/helping-teachers-manage-weight-trauma, https://traumasensitiveschools.org/. Accessed on February 16, 2019.

Newport, C. (2016). *Deep work: Rules for focused success in a distracted world.* New York: Grand Central Publishing.

Ruiz, D. M. (1997). *The four agreements.* San Rafael, CA: Amber-Allen Publishing, Inc.

Conclusion

A Few Cautionary Tales

Already you are eager to get started, or you have been a pro for a while. Wherever you are in this journey to connect and learn, it is important to recalibrate and reset limits with our uses of technology now and again.

Caution: Self-Regulating Your Time on Social Media

Have you ever plugged into your computer or your phone for just one minute, or just one thing? Only to look up and an hour has passed? Or you get sidetracked with that one website or Twitter Chat and then realize you now have more to do than when you started?

For many of us, smartphones, laptops, social media, podcasts, and other connectors were not around when we were growing up. These connectivity activities are now essential to the work we are required to do, so we not only need to learn how to use them, but learn how to set limits and step away for a while.

Newport (2016) suggests a digital detox. By scheduling when you will use the Internet and when you don't, you use your time and your mind to focus on other tasks at hand. I broke up with my phone in 2017. No really I did (blog post at the end of this chapter). By taking off all notifications, eliminating work email, and putting all my apps into one folder, I had a clean screen, and less temptation to unlock the phone to check that one thing.

Not just for productivity, but by being focused with your use of social media you might actually lower your stress levels. In Zomorodi's (2017) book, when talking with professors, she learned that the more people switch their attention, the higher the stress level. So by being over-connected you can also increase the opportunity to be over-stressed? Never mind the FOMO (fear of missing out) that accompanies most social media scrolls; switching from apps, to emails and your calendar could increase the stress in your life? How in the world can we champion change from this revelation?

Okay, there is literally an app for self-regulating your time on your phone. Moment app (Breakfree if Android) tracks how much time you are on your phone and how often you are checking it. Manoush Zomorodi offers multiple challenges and support through her book and her Bored and Brilliant challenge (www.wnyc.org/series/bored-and-brilliant) to help you set limits on the time you utilize your phone and how it takes away focus from your mind.

Change the Narrative: Sharing Gratitude and Changing the Conversation

Now that you are following a few new people, watching a few videos on YouTube, and listening to a new podcast, here is the final challenge: thank a new member of your connected tribe. The people you are following are just that, people. They have lives outside of their social media presence, they go through struggles, and learn hard lessons. Some of those you are following may post something and be shamed or shunned by their platforms. Others might be struggling through something that none of us will ever know. I share that perspective because no matter what is going on in their lives, thanking them for the work they do will always be appreciated.

Take a moment and direct message (DM) someone who has shared something with you that you have applied back in your own setting. Write a thank you to an educator that posted an idea that will impact your own learners. Go up to a presenter at a conference and thank them for the work they are sharing with others on a larger scale and for the courage it takes to stand up in the first place.

As leaders in the field, we have an opportunity and a responsibility to model respectful modes of digital citizenship for those we serve at school, and home. Don't sit silently and watch this powerful tool of connected learning be used to hurt and harm others. Speak up and share the positive things occurring in your school – and thank those who you have connected to on these platforms publicly.

Change the narrative tomorrow by thanking someone today.

 ## Conclusion: Earning the Badge

So, congrats are in order: you accepted the challenge and finished this resource. By reading this book, you answered the call; our schools need a leader who is willing to take research to practice in creative and unconventional ways.

Continue to Dream Big, Live Colorfully, and Lead Bolding in every action and interaction you take.

Want to Learn More?

Bored and Brilliant: www.wnyc.org/series/bored-and-brilliant

Cal Newport: http://calnewport.com/blog/

Newport, C. (2016). *Deep work: Rules for focused success in a distracted world.* New York: Grand Central Publishing.

Zomorodi, M. (2017). *Bored and brilliant: How spacing out can unlock your most productive and creative self.* New York: St. Martin's Press.

Appendix: So How Do I Do That?
Resources for Creating and Organizing Social Media Accounts

The trio of Todd Whitaker, Jeff Zoul, and Jimmy Casas (2015) said it best: connected educators are the ones who are actively and constantly seeking new opportunities and resources to grow as professionals. Okay, so you have taken a few notes, found a few new people in your PLN, and you are ready to try out Twitter. Below are a few of my favorite resources on getting started:

Setting up a Twitter Account

In Theresa Stager's blog post: "3 Unwritten Twitter rules when setting up your profile (so you actually get followed back!)", she states the following important pieces:

1. No egghead. Make sure you have a profile picture. It doesn't have to be perfect, but make sure it shows your leadership style, and would be something your grandma would be proud of seeing.
2. Bio. You only have a certain amount of characters so make sure they count. Linking other accounts and hashtags to your bio maximizes the characters and the message. Check out my bio: 2017 MN Principal of the Year| 2016 NAESP/VINCI Digital Leader of Early Learning| Author #HackingEarlyLearning@BalanceLAP| Principal @EllisMiddle492

Notice I used hashtags and @ to direct people to a little more about my passions and purpose to be connected with others.

3. Privacy settings. Feel free to check in with your district if you are creating a professional or school account. Checking private makes it hard for others to find you out in the social media world, and limits your connections to a new tribe.

How to Join a Twitter Chat

Just google "How to join a Twitter Chat" and you will find tons of videos, blogs, and resources that will help you get started. Here are a few simple steps.

1. Find the chat you want to participate in. Make sure you know what time zone, how long it is, and have a few ideas to share on the topic.
2. Make sure you know the right way to answer the question. I like to watch the moderator start the chat with the ground rules. Mainly the naming convention to respond to tweeted questions. Usually the response follows the same pattern:
   A1 (for Answer to question 1).
   Type your answer.
   End with the # representing the chat.
3. Listen and lean into other people's tweets. Challenge yourself to go beyond liking everything everyone else asks. Here are my challenges when I participate in a chat:
   - Respond to someone's tweet with a question to help you bring the idea into your own context.
   - Respond to someone's tweet with a GIF or an emoji when you 110% agree with what they are saying.
   - Retweet with a comment an idea that you want to share with someone else and tag them in the retweet with @__(their handle).
   - Thank the moderator at the end of the chat – trust me it is hard work to maintain a conversation for a period of time on Twitter – and they will appreciate the moment of gratitude.

Want a little more information? This is one of my favorites from one of the very best in our educational PLN. Cool Cat Teacher: How to join a Twitter Chat: www.youtube.com/watch?v=ayfu0s3ypX4

 ## How to Organize Twitter Followers and Hashtags

Hopefully throughout the book you found a few hashtags you are curious about following. Well, if you are not into grazing your feed to find new tweets, utilize the list function on Twitter. Twitter has a nice tutorial on how to get started. I have around ten different lists ranging from early learning leaders to a list of just educators on Twitter from my district. I can click into that list and catch up on what they have been up to without having to scroll through my whole feed.

TweetDeck. Another great tool to utilize is TweetDeck. TweetDeck allows you to see multiple accounts, hashtags across your computer screen. I usually have my TweetDeck up when I am on social media as it is a quick way to glance across my lists and see what is new, relevant, and applicable to what I am looking for or who I want to connect with at the time.

IFTTT. Do you have a school Facebook, Twitter, and Instagram account? Tired of posting the same information three separate times? If That Then This (get it IFTTT) utilizes a recipe (or applets) to trigger an action. So, you can create an applet that triggers as soon as you post to Twitter and then it posts the same thing to Instagram and Facebook! I bet you have seen some of your PLN already using this tool. Curious? Check out my Instagram (JessicaCabeen) and my Jessica Cabeen Facebook page: www.facebook.com/PrincipalinBalance/ and see how it works.

 ## Branding Your Message

Once you get started, finding a hashtag for your school, or your own personal mantra, is a way to organize your social media posts and to promote your school and message. Work with a team (students included) to create a hashtag – remember the fewer characters the easier to remember and capitalization doesn't matter. Check out your choices by searching to see if anyone is already using them and then get to work promoting the work. Include the brand on your email signature line, on school materials, and commit to posting using the hashtag at least three times per week.

From Overwhelmed to Organized: How to Start "Connecting" in 10 minutes Per Day

Okay, let's do this! You are motivated, you are in the know, and ready to go! Try jumping into this connected world in small bites with intentional purpose for your searching and then grow. This plan requires you to set aside 10 minutes a day to start dipping into the waters.

- Choose an adventure:
  - Pick a hashtag that you have identified in the end of chapter challenge and:
    - Like one post.
    - Retweet one idea.
    - Comment on one picture and ask a question about how they are accomplishing the work.
    - Comeback tomorrow and check out your notifications to see the responses.
  - Find and follow one of the #UnConLeaders from the book.
    - Comment on a recent post.
    - Retweet with a comment about a recent blog post, graphic, or something else on their feed that resonates with you and the work you are accomplishing.
    - Comment and tag another friend to get connected with an idea, an article, or something else that they would utilize as well in their work.
  - Spend a few minutes on one of your favorite blogs, news feeds, or email blasts from your leadership organizations.
    - Find an article of interest and tweet it out (most platforms now have a Twitter bird near the top of the resource to make this easy to share).
    - Add a comment, hashtag, or way for you to come back and remember why you posted it to your page.

Find/subscribe to a blog. Blogs are a great way to find out more from other educators and learn from them on a regular basis. Once you find a blog you like, look on the home page to subscribe to the blog. When a new post comes out you will be notified via email and can stay current in what your fellow friends are up to on a regular basis.

Find/subscribe to a podcast. Similar to a blog, once you find a podcast you like you can subscribe to it and receive updates to when new ones are released.

Creating amazing graphics. If you have been on Twitter, you have seen those great graphics people pull together with quotes, questions, and chats. If you think that they have professional designers creating those graphics – think again. Many of these can be created for free, and from your phone. My two go-to tools are www.canva.com/ and https://spark.adobe.com – these tools are easy to navigate and fun to use.

#BookSnaps. A new tool I have used to enhance my Twitter game is actually … Snapchat. After following Tara Martin for years and her hashtag #BookSnaps I started an account and got to work. My goal – one #BookSnap per week, and I post it outside of my office with the book I am currently reading. It has started some great conversations – not just about what I am reading, but newly found Snapchat skills with the middle schoolers.

Finding a Voxer tribe. Voxer is one of my favorite ways to connect with my PLN. I can still remember when I first started connecting on Voxer and totally geeking out when Dr. Brad Gustafson responded to a Voxer message I sent! Since then I have enjoyed hearing the voices and having conversations with members of my PLN in small settings and large groups. Mark Barnes has put together a great slide deck on the power of this tool: www.slideshare.net/markbarnes19/create-your-tribe-with-voxer.

Educators use this tool for creating school groups, sending voice messages after walkthroughs, or even communicating with their own family. The bonus to this tool is it can be used on your phone or on your desktop making it accessible in multiple formats.

How to Implement Research into Practice

Are you ready to dig a little deeper into this work with an intentional lens? Just googling trends such as flexible seating, scheduling, personalized learning, grading practices, formative assessments, trauma

informed, and reading well by 3rd grade will fill
your feed with resources, opinion papers, and
even teacher pay teacher accounts of activities. But
before you dive into implementation, taking a step
back to review the research and implement well will make a difference
down the road.

1. **What is your focus?** Narrowing your field to search is essential.
   Is the topic a K-12 implication but you really only want to focus
   on grades 4 and 5? Is there a subpopulation you are focusing
   on to pilot a new learning strategy? Be as specific as you can to
   start so the research you use is aligned to the work you want to
   accomplish.
2. **Find the resources**. For me this is the fun part. As a member of
   NASSP, NAESP, and ASCD I have articles and journals literally at
   my fingertips. Searching archives on their websites have afforded
   me trusted research and implementation models to consider. From
   those articles I use the index and resources they cite to see if those
   would be important to include in our work.
3. **Form a team**. Now you have resources including articles, books,
   and blogs. At this point it is time to pull a team together to help
   read and interpret the information. All my committees have been
   volunteer based, and usually have a targeted start and stop date. In
   my career we have had teams for some of the following topics: writing in preK/K, establishing PLCs, creating essential outcomes, SEL
   curriculum, grading practices in the middle school, and standards
   based IEPs in the secondary grades. Offering some resources and
   allowing the team to go out and seek more brings a greater diversity
   to the group and a wider breadth of research to draw from in the
   work.
4. **Start with the why**. Before you get into the details of practice, take
   the time to define the why of the work. I reference Simon Sinek's
   work and YouTube videos to ground the committee in ensuring
   we are doing the right things for the right reasons with the right
   research. Plan to spend the first meeting fully devoted to the why
   of the work before jumping into the how and what.
5. **Share your resources**. When your committee is ready to make a
   recommendation, pilot a strategy, or seek input from the school

make sure to cite and share the resources that guided the work. By being transparent, and showing what you learned, you build a base of trust with the school as you didn't make decisions in isolation but in collaboration from research and other schools in practice.

6. **Reflect and review**. Never make this work a one and done. Revisit the work throughout the year and set more in-depth review cycles to ensure the work you started is appropriate to sustain 5–10 years from now.

Want to Learn More?

Cabeen, J. (2017, July 18). Breaking up with your phone. [Blog Post] Retrieved from https://principalinbalance.wordpress.com/2017/07/18/breaking-up-with-your-phone/. Accessed on March 10, 2019.

Stager, T. (2017, June 30). 3 Unwritten Twitter rules when setting up your profile (so you actually get followed back!) [Blog post] Retrieved from: www.principalstager.com/twitterrules/. Accessed on February 17, 2019.

Whitaker, T., Zoul, J., & Casas, J. (2015). *What connected educators do differently*. New York: Routledge.